KOINANGE-WA-MBIYU

KOINANGE-WA-MBIYU

MAU MAU'S MISUNDERSTOOD LEADER

Jeff M. Koinange

The Book Guild Ltd
Sussex, England

B KOINANGE-WA-MBIYU

This book is sold subject to the condition that it shall not, by way of trade or otherwise, be lent, re-sold, hired out, photocopied or held in any retrieval system or otherwise circulated without the publisher's prior consent in any form of binding or cover other than that in which this is published and without a similar condition including this condition being imposed on the subsequent purchaser.

The Book Guild Ltd
25 High Street,
Lewes, Sussex

First published 2000
© Jeff M. Koinange, 2000

Set in Times
Typesetting by Keyboard Services, Luton

Printed in Great Britain by
Bookcraft (Bath) Ltd, Avon

A catalogue record for this book is
available from the British Library

ISBN 1 85776 412 9

CONTENTS

Preface		vii
Foreword		ix
Acknowledgements		xiii
Koinange-wa-Mbiyu Family Genealogy		xvi
Introduction		xix
Chapter 1	Land of Mongai and Mumbi	1
Chapter 2	Coming of Age	6
Chapter 3	Searching for a Wife	14
Chapter 4	Forced Removal from Ancestral Home	19
Chapter 5	Politics of Participation	33
Chapter 6	Taking a Stand	45
Chapter 7	Mbiyu Abroad	58
Chapter 8	Signs of a Revolution	72
Chapter 9	State of Emergency	87
Chapter 10	The Detention Years	97
Chapter 11	Coming Home to Die	107
Endnotes		116
Bibliography		122
Glossary		124

PREFACE

I first began research on this project more than six years ago, after brushing past the Carl Rosberg/John Nottingham book, *The Myth of Mau Mau*, in the library at New York University. The fact that the subject of Africa's most violent testament to colonial rule was being discussed so openly in books there in the United States further fuelled my desire to see how our people in general and our family in particular were being portrayed. The more I read about this subject the more I realised that too many brave men and women went unmentioned, and too many of them never received credit for their heroic deeds. I hope this will help make people aware that *Mau Mau* was less about rituals and oaths and more about freedom and land rights and a people's desire to rise up in the face of insurmountable oppression.

There are, of course, people who are going to disagree with some of the content; that's par for the course. I've tried to portray the incidents as accurately as I can, based on extensive research and interviews with family members as well as reliable eyewitness accounts. One has to keep in mind that with a subject like *Mau Mau*, which is over a half-century old, the reliance on eyewitness accounts is crucial to get as close as possible to the truth.

Some family members aren't going to be pleased with the way they've been depicted; all I can say is that every fact and figure has been checked and double-checked, and if I've caused anyone any kind of mental or physical despair I take full responsibility.

What's most important and what we all have to keep in mind is that the man I've focused my research on is probably one of the foremost reasons why we are where we are as Kenyans today. What I hope to accomplish is to give him the credit he rightfully deserves while at the same time clear up any kind of doubt as to what his role really was in the movement that came to be known as *Mau Mau*. Hopefully, we can all learn from the cruel and harsh lessons our forefathers were forced to endure. Let us also keep in mind that even though history has an uncanny habit of repeating itself, it is our hope that we will never have to suffer the way they did.

Footnotes throughout refer to the Bibliography on page 122.

FOREWORD
BY MARSHALL S. CLOUGH

In an important respect, the history of modern Kenya is family history and community history. Historians know, whether they are working in the archives or interviewing in the field, that every name encountered and every personality mentioned needs then to be placed in the complex web of kin and neighbour relationships that composes the Kenyan social world. (See, for example, the genealogy at the beginning of this book.) In Kiambu District, the lineage of Mbari ya Njunu has occupied a prominent place for more than six generations. There is little doubt that during this period of time the most remarkable member of Mbari ya Njunu has been Koinange wa Mbiyu, and Koinange should be remembered not only as an outstanding representative of his lineage but also of Kiambu, the Gikuyu, and Kenyans as a whole.

The life of Koinange wa Mbiyu, ably told in this biography by his grandson Jeff Koinange, is both an inspiring and tragic story. Koinange exemplifies a type of African leader during the first half of the twentieth century, the kind of leader who attempted to reconcile working under the British and serving his people at the same time. While he accepted British appointment to the chieftaincy, converted to Christianity, and adopted European farming methods on his land, Koinange also protested against land alienation, called for wider educational opportunities for Gikuyu children, and agitated for African political rights. He served as the president of the Kikuyu Association from its founding in 1919 and later became a leader of the Kikuyu

Central Association. His advocacy of his people's cause in the 1920s and 1930s won the strong support of the Kiambu community and the respect of Gikuyu opponents on his left. It also aroused the suspicion of British district commissioners – men who had worked closely with Koinange and valued his abilities but were officially intolerant of chiefs who took their role as mediators too seriously.

By the late 1940s, frustrated by British indifference to reform, Koinange turned to clandestine action as the leader of political oath-taking in Kiambu. Under his direction and at his home, hundreds of people from Kiambu and Nairobi took the oath of the secret movement. After the assassination of his erstwhile friend and present antagonist Chief Waruhiu wa Kung'u in October of 1952 – the political killing that persuaded the government to declare a State of Emergency – Koinange wa Mbiyu and members of his family were arrested for murder. Although he was acquitted of involvement in the assassination for lack of evidence, the British detained Koinange under Emergency regulations for seven years, disregarding his long service as a chief. The archival record detailing the conditions of his detention and the struggle of his family and allies in Britain and the United States (especially Fenner Brockway and Ralph Bunche) to win his release makes depressing reading. The British only lifted Koinange's detention when he fell seriously ill. He lived long enough at home for many Gikuyu from all over Central Kenya to visit him before he died, and his funeral in 1960 was a public occasion attended by thousands.

Jeff Koinange makes strong claims for his grandfather's importance in the leadership ranks of the Mau Mau movement. Since the publication in 1966 of Rosberg's and Nottingham's pioneering academic study – a book which Jeff Koinange tells us first piqued his interest in writing about Mau Mau himself – dozens of articles and books have been written by Kenyan and foreign scholars, by novelists, by journalists, and by Mau Mau veterans. Much has come to light, and we are now more familiar with Mau Mau in the Rift Valley, Nairobi, and Kiambu, and with Mau Mau oath-taking, organizing, and fighting. Yet in some respects the essential nature of Mau Mau as a whole remains elusive, controversial. These writings have not simplified our understanding of Mau Mau; indeed, it could be said that they have actually revealed the considerable complexity of the secret movement.

The historiography reflects on the role of Koinange wa Mbiyu in Mau Mau. Some of the recently published accounts point toward a Mau Mau movement that took on different aspects, not only at different times but in different parts of the country. Most writers on the subject would agree that Koinange's leadership was of critical importance in Kiambu when the clandestine movement was born, when the oaths were first administered, when activists laid the first plans for confrontation with the British. They could also assert that even in this formative period there were other foci for secret action (Nairobi, Nyeri, the Rift Valley), and could point out that the arrest of Koinange at the very beginning of the war itself shunted him aside into detention for most of the Emergency (as did the arrests of Jomo Kenyatta and Bildad Kaggia). However, as a leading patriot, even in his absence Koinange continued during the war to inspire the men and women who fought the British in the districts, in the forests, and in the towns. Jeff Koinange's biography can help foreign and Kenyan historians, other Kenyan citizens, and members of Koinange's kin keep his memory fresh, both of his role as a leader during colonial rule and as a fighter for independence. The contrast with more recent leadership, moreover, is telling and instructive.

This life story is not only about politics, however. The early chapters, partly drawn from the rich trove of the Ralph Bunche papers at the University of California at Los Angeles, are full of interesting details of traditional Gikuyu social life. Koinange's childhood experiences herding goats for his family, particularly his participation in the herdsboys' playfighting and dances, are vividly brought to life. There is an absorbing description of the circumcision ceremony. The description of Koinange's betrothal to his first wife, Wambui d/o Kihara, is replete with information on Gikuyu marriage customs near the turn of the last century. The betrothal was poignantly interrupted by the devastating great famine of the 1890s (usually called Ng'aragu ya Ruraya, the 'famine of Europe'), a disaster which marked the beginning of a new and difficult period of the long Gikuyu history.

This biography is not intended to be a scholarly work. Jeff Koinange has used archives, conducted interviews, and consulted professional histories, but he has kept the academic apparatus to a minimum. This is appropriate. Like Jeremy Murray-Brown, the biographer of Kenyatta, Koinange is an experienced journalist, who has worked for the Kenya Television Network, for Reuters, and for other news services. His book is valuable to historians like myself, but it was written to be accessible to the general reader.

Jeff Koinange graciously acknowledges my help in the preface, and I would like to provide a little background to this. I first became interested in the life and career of Koinange wa Mbiyu during my doctoral research on early Kenyan nationalism in 1973–1974. Fieldwork involved more than fifty interviews (including some with Koinange's family, including his son Charles Karuga Koinange) and in almost every interview in Kiambu my informants spoke warmly of Koinange, sometimes at length. I soon realized that he had been both a pivotal figure in the politics of colonial Kenya and a man of considerable standing within Kiambu society. Later I came to discuss his career at length in my book *Fighting Two Sides: Kenyan Chiefs and Politicians, 1918–1940*, and also had the opportunity to write a chapter entitled '*Koinange wa Mbiyu: Mediator and Patriot*' for the collection *Biographical Essays in Imperialism and Collaboration in Colonial Kenya*, edited by B. E. Kipkorir. At one time I hoped to write a book on Koinange, but I became involved in other projects, and was very pleased when Jeff Koinange contacted me in 1993, told me that he had read my work, and asked for his help in writing a biography of his grandfather. Over the last six years I and others have offered him advice and read versions of the manuscript. The research and writing have inevitably taken a while, sandwiched as they have had to be into the busy career of a professional journalist. I am delighted that Jeff Koinange's book has at last come to publication. This biography is both an effort of familial devotion and a document in the preservation of modern Kenya's history.

ACKNOWLEDGEMENTS

There are a lot of people I'd like to thank without whom this project would never have gotten off the ground. Firstly, I'd like to thank God for making all this possible. Secondly, my mother, Mary Mbiyu Koinange, who refused to re-marry even after losing her husband when she was only 29 years old and despite being ostracised by many of her in-laws. Thanks too to Jan Hemsing, without whom I'd have given up with frustration at going through the manuscript over and over again, to Professor Marshall S. Clough for his advice and kind words as well as his knowledge of research and writing, to Jeff Rankin at the University of California photo library for painstakingly going through literally hundreds of negatives and selecting the photos seen inside, and to all the other people who helped in one way or another, especially family members who gave their insight into this great man and who've enabled his name to live forever.

'A noble person goes on his way
Conscious of his nobility.'

> Hampton Institute
> Class of '31

KOINANGE-WA-MBIYU FAMILY (Patriarch)

(Family Geneaology)

MARIAM WAMBUI (1st wife)	JULIA NJERI (2nd wife)	JOYCE KAGENDO (3rd wife)	PHYLLIS WAMBUI (4th wife)	ELIZABETH GATHONI (5th wife)	BEATRICE GATAA (6th wife)
I Wanjiku/Githaria	J Mbiyu/P Njogu	E Wanjiku/N Itote	P Wanjiku/	M Wanjiku/	L Gacambi/E Muiruri
P Wambui	P Koinange	Kagwe	Njoroge	E Gathoni	
R Nyambura	J Njeri	H Wanjiru	I Koinange	I Koinange	
A Njenga		Gathecha	Wambui	Mbiyu	
C Nyawera					
L Wairimu	T Wanjiku/				
	Mwaura	D Gathiomi/D Wanjiru	E Mbiyu/Nyambura	W Mbiyu	
P Mbiyu/L Njeri (1st wife)	J Njoroge	W Koinange	I Koinange	E Gathoni	
D Njunu	Wambui	J Wambui	Kinuthia	I Koinange	
D Mbatia	Njeri	F Njeri	Karuga	Wangui	
M Wambui	Koinange	Njoroge	Wambui	Njehia	
G Kihara		Wanjiku		Ngethe	
E Waruinu	J Njoroge/D Thetu				
I Wanjiku	Koinange		R Njenga/B Gathoni	P Wambui/Malu	
	F Ndegwa	F Mbiyu/M Nyambura	I Koinange	D Koinange	
P Mbiyu/D Wambui (2nd wife)	J Mbiyu	H Wanjiru	P Wambui	V Malu	
I Njunu	R Muthoni	P Wangi	Wamwiri	J Gathoni	
F Wanjiku	M Njeri	F Koinange			
D Waiganjo	G Ikuro	J Mwaura (author)			
S Kihara	Karuga		Wamueii/Muchiri	G Tharuba	
G Karuga	Gachiku		Nyambura	E Gathoni	
L Wanjiku			I Koinange	I Koinange	

L Wairimu/O Kariuki
Virginia
M Wambui
J Chinga
D Koinange
J Nganga
Ndiku
M Wanjiku
Mbiyu
P Nyariru
E Mbatia
P Kihara

E Wanjama/
R Nyambura
J Njeri
Koinange
Waithera
Gikuiyu
Njoroge
Wanjiku

N Karuga/J Muthoni
(1st wife)
P Koinange
F Mbiyu

G Wairimu/
Ndegwa
I Koinange
Wambui

I Wairimu
O Njoroge
Gitau

N Karuga/G Ngina
(2nd wife)
N Koinange
W Machua
A Wanjiru

Karuamba/
Wainaina
I Koinange

L Karuga/
I Koinange
E Gathoni
Wambui

J Karuga/G Njeri
J Njeri
D Koinange

M Wangui/J Gecau
J Gecau
Wanjiku
Wanjiru

G Wanjiru/
E Gathoni

L Wairimu/Muchiri
Wairimu

I Wairimu (died in detention)

C Karuga/Nduta
(1st wife)
Wanduga
J Wambui
Kangethe
M Wanjira
W Kihara
M Wambui
E Ngugi
R Gichuki

C Karuga/M Njoki
(2nd wife)
J Wambui
Koinange
W Wamagata
F Mbiyu

H Wariara/N Chege
S Nyambura
Koinanage
R Wanjiku
C Muthoni
M Wambui
Jeremiah

A Karuamba/G Wamute
Waruingi
M Kibui
Koinange
E Kanyi

G Mitundu/J Kenyatta
Jane Njeri (later Jane Gecaga)

Bold denotes: Koinange-wa-Mbiyu's children

INTRODUCTION

Before we explore the life of Koinange-wa-Mbiyu, it's important to first understand the situation as it was in the late 19th century and the European powers' so-called 'scramble for Africa'.

The abolition of the slave trade in the late 1840s allowed commerce and trade to prosper along the West African coast. Until 1860, the Europeans were generally unwilling to extend protectorates over Africans, as that would have required additional expenditures. In fact, in 1843 the African Committee of the British House of Commons passed a resolution expressing Britain's reluctance to further engage in colonial affairs. This, however, did not last very long. Growing commercial competition forced the British to reconsider their position or face being squeezed out of Africa. Throughout the second half of the 19th century the British, French, Dutch, Belgians, Portuguese and others brutishly jostled one another for influence and control over the trade of certain valued commodities. They built forts and castles – especially along the West African coast – not only to defend their commercial interests against foreign interlopers, but to expand trade. To secure commercial advantages, they signed friendship treaties with chiefs and kings.

So intense was the competition for commercial hegemony that in 1884 the German Chancellor, Prince Otto von Bismarck, convened a conference of European nations with the avowed purpose of reducing tensions among them. The effect of the conference was to establish rules for recognising what they termed 'spheres of influence'. A frenetic scramble ensued to establish such spheres of dominance where none had existed before.

It's been argued by historians that the roots of the scramble may have begun some 15 years earlier in particular in the war between France and Prussia that led to the loss by France of large regions and to the proclamation of the German empire at Versailles in 1871.

A humiliated France faced a new Germany, powerful but not completely convinced of its security. In the decade-and-a-half that followed, Bismarck, the master diplomat, wanted to divert France's attention from the recovery of its lost provinces.

The old empires of Portugal and Britain and the emerging new empires of Italy and Belgium were, of necessity, involved in the attempt to keep the balance of power in Germany's hands. The emerging industrially based economies throughout Europe sought new markets, areas of capital investment, and sources of raw materials overseas. Africa, with its vast, fertile lands and rich resources, was a convenient field into which this political and economic imbroglio of Europe could extend itself.

Although Africa's interior by the 1880s had been charted in considerable detail by European explorers, those parts that were in doubt provided excellent sources of speculation for the powers of Europe, especially Germany, France, Britain and Portugal.

Tendentious treaties were extorted from African rulers, in some cases by sheer military force. De facto protectorates became colonies almost overnight. Various rationales were proffered to justify colonialisation, but the one group of people who never had a say nor were consulted in the matter were the Africans themselves. One claim was that 'African savages' needed to be civilised to be freed from the oppressive regimes of their traditional rulers.

Bismarck's convening of the Berlin Conference had, no doubt, more than enough of the characteristically Machiavellian motivations of the Iron Chancellor. But his ostensible objective – and that of the powers represented at the conference – was to prevent a European war. Much that happened around the conference table at Berlin and in back-room bargaining in those

13 weeks in 1884–85 no doubt made more certain the scramble for African territory and concessions by the powers of Europe. It could be argued that it prevented a European war in the late 1880s, but only at the expense of partitioning and balkanising Africa and, ultimately, of ensuring the emergence of a major European war at a later date.

The personal empire of King Leopold II of Belgium no doubt profited most notably from the Berlin Conference. Its general act led to Leopold's recognition as sovereign head of the Congo Free State. The checking of British and Portuguese expansion in West and East Africa, French gains in West Africa, and the triumph of Bismarckian diplomacy were also important results.

The cunning and avaricious Belgian king took every advantage through his own tortuous brand of diplomacy of the requirements of the conference: that claims to colonies and protectorates on any part of the African coastline should be formally notified to the other powers that took part in the Berlin Conference and that such claims must be backed by an effective degree of authority. The calling in Brussels in 1890 of a second international conference on Africa to regularise and humanise the partition was used by Leopold to make a breach in the free-trade provisions of the Berlin Conference – to the advantage of his Congo possessions. By 1890, the Congo Independent State, a vast area 80 times the size of Belgium, was a reality under the absentee regime of King Leopold.

In 1895, five European super powers – Britain, France, Germany, Italy and Portugal – met in Versailles to discuss how to divide the continent of Africa into what came to be known as 'spheres of influence'. By 1898, the scramble for the greater part of Africa was largely complete. The French had taken the lion's share of territory, particularly in the north, the Sahara regions and West Africa. But Britain was not without compensations in west Africa From the existing coastal possessions, especially in the north, extended an already sizeable empire.

Germany, meanwhile, taking advantage of the bargaining positions obtained by Bismarck emerged from the scramble with a considerable portion of the continent It spread-eagled across from Togo and Cameroon in West Africa, through the extensive possessions of German South-West Africa to German East Africa. The latter's common borders with what later became the British colonies of British East Africa (Kenya) and Uganda were defined in a series of agreements in 1890.

African resistance to colonial rule was in general weak because of the vast superiority of European weapons. In particular, the Maxim gun proved decisive. Frequently, African armies of 30,000 or more were routed by European-led armies of a tenth the size or less. Such victories bred over-confidence and caused the Europeans to surmise erroneously that the weak resistance was due to the oppression of Africans by their rulers.

The Europeans thus overestimated their welcome and acceptance. All in all, the early colonial years brought political subjugation and humiliation to Africans. Scores of African rulers died on the battlefield; many more were executed or exiled after defeat. Those who signed treaties and remained protected rulers soon found themselves demoted from king to chief and were required to collect taxes or recruit labourers for their British, French or German overlords.

Though Africa was conquered with relative military ease, the cultural battle proved far more formidable and costly than the Europeans had anticipated. It was one thing to subjugate a people and demand obedience and taxes by military force. But it was quite another to force them to shed centuries-old traditions, to adopt alien ways of doing things, and to respond willingly to the dictates of a foreign culture.

1

Land of Mongai and Mumbi

Kikuyuland stretches over an area of about 100 miles from north to south and about 50 miles from east to west. The massive bulk of Mount Kenya marks the northern boundary, the Ngong Hills the southern, the Aberdare Range and the Kikuyu Escarpment mark the western boundary, and the slopes of Embu mark the eastern borderline.

According to folklore, the tribe first established its home around Nyaga, the 'mountain of mystery', otherwise known as Mount Kenya, home of Mwene Nyaga, the supernatural power, the possessor of mystery or whiteness, who was their tribal high God. Tradition has it that it was on this mountain that Mwene Nyaga appeared to the first man, Gekoyo or Gikuyu, the founder of the tribe. He took Gikuyu to the top of the mountain, among the glittering snow-covered peaks where no man had ever set foot, and showed him the beauty of the surrounding country. The rivers sparkled in the sun, herds of antelope and other beasts, great and small, grazed contentedly on the grassy plains, and a cool breeze swept over the forest trees with a pleasant rustling sound. Gikuyu's heart was filled with joy, for Mwene Nyaga was generous to him, and he saw that the country was well-watered with numerous rivers and streams of pure and clear water. It was forested with fine cedar, olive, bamboo and other trees, and the open spaces were carpeted with springy turf. The scene was made more beautiful by a circle of high mountains surrounding the country on east, south, west and north. Looking far away to the horizon, he could see these mountains rising skyward, like an immense wall along which, here and there, rose clusters of domed buildings, so that the whole country looked like a gigantic well-protected homestead.

When Gikuyu had surveyed it he lifted his hands and, with his eyes fixed on Mwene Nyaga, proclaimed, 'O my father, Great Elder, I have no words to thank you, but with your deep wisdom I am sure that you can see how I value your glorious gifts. O my father, when I look upon your greatness, I am filled with awe. O Great Elder, ruler of all things earthly and heavenly, I am your warrior, ready to act in accordance with your will.'[1]

Mwene Nyaga turned to him and said, 'My good and brave warrior, your words have touched my heart and I am pleased. Within these walls your sons and daughters shall roam and multiply, enjoying at the same time the fruits thereof, and always remembering that it is I who have bestowed them upon you. My blessing shall be with you and your offspring wherever you go.'[2]

Then he commanded Gikuyu to descend and build his homestead in a certain place surrounded by fig trees (*mekoyo*). Soon afterwards Mwene Nyaga gave him a wife whom he named Moombi (the creator or moulder). They lived happily together and had nine daughters, but no sons. Gikuyu wanted to found a family to inherit the good land, and remembering Mwene Nyaga's words about his sons and daughters who should roam the countryside, he approached him. Mwene Nyaga told him to make a sacrifice at a certain spot in a sacred grove, and then go away, and come back when the lamb which he had offered was all burnt up. He did so, and there beside the embers of the fire stood nine young men, who offered themselves as bridegrooms for his daughters. There was great rejoicing when he took them home, and they were accepted, but only on condition that they should all live together in one village around his homestead, and that the women should be the heads of their households. So it came about that the nine clans of the Gikuyu tribe were founded, and took their names from the nine daughters of Gikuyu: Wacheera, Wanjiko, Wairimu, Wamboi, Wangare, Wanjiro, Wangoi, Mwethaga (Warigia) and Waithera.[3]

The tribe continued to multiply until there came a time for it to separate. It did so into three main divisions: Gikuyu proper, the Meru and the Wakamba. These kept the traditions of their common origin, but formed independent communities, each with its own government.

The Wakamba moved south-eastward, following the Tana River, in search of more fertile land or of better grazing grounds. They increased, until eventually they formed a people in themselves, distinct from the Gikuyu. Two outstanding features remain to identify them with the main body of the Gikuyu: the similarity in their language, and the fundamental principles of their customs and traditions.

The Meru, on the other hand, moved northward. There they formed a separate local group, rather than a tribe, and developed a dialect which, though it is intelligible to the other sections, has many characteristics of its own. But they never became a separate people like the Wakamba; in all tribal affairs they remained closely allied to the Gikuyu. As time went on the Gikuyu proper divided themselves into two main sections. The more adventurous moved gradually southward, while the central section remained around the foothills of Kere Nyaga. The southern group are known as the Karura, or Kabete, and the cental group as the Moranga, Mathera, Ndia and Embu. There seems to have been no attempt to push further to the west of the mountain. This must have been mainly due to the presence of the Purko Maasai who lived in this area at the time.

Nyeri, Muranga (formerly known as Fort Hall, after the British pioneer, Francis Hall) and Kiambu are the administrative districts of this Gikuyuland. While they were created in the early 1900s as purely a matter of convenience for the settlers, their common boundaries were recognized as territorial units before the coming of the British. Kiambu district, the Southernmost of the three, begins at Chania River and runs to the outskirts of Nairobi, a distance of about 35 kilometers.

The natural vegetation of Gikuyuland is mainly forest with scatterings of grass and bush. The area receives abundant rainfall (during the two rainy seasons of March-May and October-December) and is blessed with moderate temperatures and rich soil. In colonial times, these advantages enabled the Gikuyu to be self sufficient in food production with surplus harvests going to trading with neighbouring tribes. Cash crops such as coffee and tea were supplemented with food crops like maize, yams, beans and bananas and sweet potatoes.[4]

The socio-political system that evolved within this setting recognised a hierarchy of blood, age and sex, but contained democratic and egalitarian strains as well. Throughout the pre-colonial period, Gikuyu society was held together by kinship, residence and association.

The kin members of related nuclear and extended families lived together as a lineage, *mbari*, on the lineage estate, *githaka*; the members of a lineage might number from a few dozen people up to several thousand, and their estate could measure 100 acres or so. Residence proximity was a bond for unrelated neighbours, and residents of contiguous homesteads or dwellers on the same ridge would cooperate to help each other.

More important than residence, however, in bringing together unrelated Gikuyu were the associations; that is, the age-grades and age-sets. The age-grades corresponded to successive stages in a person's life; a man, for example, entered the warrior grade after circumcision and the elder grade after marriage and the birth of his first child.

A person always remained in the same age-set, however, because his or her *riika* was determined by the year of circumcision. The age-grades and age-sets cut across kin division in pre-colonial Gikuyu society and helped provide a degree of social cohesion.[5]

Political authority in pre-colonial Kenya was decentralised. There was no such thing as Kings or chiefs and institutions as we know them, never existed. For the most part, political authority was collective at every level, from the *riika* to the *Mbari* and decisions were generally taken by the eldest males of the *Mbari* in the *kiama*.

While the *kiamas* made important decisions for the group, their main role was in settling disputes between warring or antagonistic *Mbaris*. Women also had their own separate but reasonably equal council know as *kiama kia atumia* whose function was to deal mainly with domestic matters pertaining to the home and the tilling of the land as well as other matters relating to female social life. Since women traditionally had no rights of land ownership, they were excluded from politics in general.[6]

The fluid social and political situation in the Kiambu frontier had enabled strong Gikuyu individuals to acquire untraditional powers, thus aiding the British in dividing and conquering the people of the district. The establishment of the Kiambu chieftaincy brought the fluid situation to an end.

As the local representatives of the British government, the early Kiambu chiefs had various duties, not to benefit their people, but to control them and make them available to the white ruling class. They were expected to keep order in their areas and control the young warriors; they were in charge of bringing revenue from taxes and fines; they were required to provide porters for officials on tour in the localities; they were expected to encourage men and women to work on settler farms; and they acted as court judges, settling disputes.

2

Coming of Age

He was born Njunu-wa-Mbiyu or Gathecha on a date that fell between 1878 and 1881, scion to a wealthy land-owning lineage known as Mbari-ya-Njunu. The lineage was established by his great-grandfather, who had come to Kamiti near Kiambaa from Mangu in southern Kiambu. When Njuno died he left all his land to his son, Gikonyo, who in turn left it to his son, Gathecha. Gathecha left it to his son, Mbiyu, the father of Koinange. His given name, Gathecha, comes from a custom that dictates that the first-born son takes the name of his father's father and the first-born daughter the name of the father's mother.[1] Legend has it that he was given the name Koinange from the Kikuyu verb, *kunanga*, which literally means 'to break' because he was so good at breaking or solving people's problems.[2] The other theory has it that the name was given to him because he was such an expert at dancing and Koinange was the name of a dance of which he was very fond.[3]

His mother was born at what is now Riara Estate, then called *Ichangiri*, by the Riara River. Her father was Karuga-wa-Muturi from the powerful and wealthy Agachiku clan. Koinange's father was also of the Agachiku clan and was an important man as leader of the warriors.[4]

In a land where the clan system controlled distribution of land, the Gathecha clan was very powerful. Weaker clans used to make 'treaties' with them for protection. When the weaker clan joined the stronger one, to be readied for war, their warriors were feasted on oxen.

Young Koinange's earliest recollection was herding goats for his father. This was the custom for boys who had yet to be circumcised. His father taught him to separate sheep from goats and how to distinguish between the colours of the sheep. Each animal was given a name according to the colour or the cuts (branding) it had on its ears. Every night when he got home, he had to select those that went to his mother's hut (females) and those that went to his father's (males). If an animal was missing, he would be punished.

The father did the branding, until the sons were old enough to do it He remembers that times were very dangerous then, due to the presence of wild animals in the area.

'I once had trouble with a leopard over a goat. The leopard seized one of my father's goats as I struggled to hold on to its hind legs. At the same time I began shouting for help, and my age-mates, who were also herding goats nearby, ran to see what the commotion was about. This startled the leopard, who took off into the bushes, leaving its dead prey. When my father heard about this incident he was very proud of me and rewarded me by giving me a goat for myself as well as more responsibilities.'[5]

He also recalls that this leopard incident occurred a little after a 'ghost-man' had passed through his village on the way to Nyeri, in the Central Highlands, the first white man ever to set eyes on this part of the country.

'The people were so surprised to see this ghost-child, white like a baby, that they slaughtered sheep and smeared the blood over their eyes. They saw white and thought that it was a deformity he had been born with. The European's name was Count Teleki, and when he smoked people thought he had fire coming out of his stomach. We were very afraid of his colour. He stayed at my grandfather's (Gathecha) village, and a goat was slaughtered and its blood drawn. There was also an Arab with the European and at Gathecha's suggestion, they took some of his blood and some from one of Gathecha's sons, and smeared each other and a piece of the goat's skin was put on the wrist of the German, the Arab, Gathecha and one of his sons. This was to make peace.'[6]

Teleki brought with him gifts of wires, bracelets, brass and beads, and he in turn was given fat rams, after which he was escorted part of the way to the Ruiru River and there handed over to the next village, thus allowing the expedition safe passage.

In the meantime the young boys learned how to make huts by building small rainshelter huts for themselves. They were taught by the older circumcised boys who were herding with them. The younger boys were also taught to cultivate plots of land, *shambas*, using skills they'd need when they became older. At the time of his birth and early childhood, Koinange's people were engaged in wars against the Maasai. As he grew older, war gave way to dances and these were very popular. The uncircumcised boys had their dances, called *ngocho*. The older, circumcised boys had theirs, called *gichukia*. Dances between boys and girls were known as *ndirii*. The herdsboys' daily lives therefore consisted of dancing and practising warfare. They would strip bark from a tree to fashion shields and use long sticks for spears and wooden swords. They would form groups and play a sort of hide and seek. The play-fighting of the herdsboys was called *ithako*, and the fighting often got very rough. Participants got hurt regularly, but usually not severely. The herdsboys also engaged in whistle-blowing or *mutorireo*. They also practised the art of whistle calls to each other, as well as specific whistle signals for cows, goats and sheep.

According to Gikuyu custom it was left to the mother to teach girls and warn them how serious it was to have intercourse before circumcision. If it was discovered that a girl had had sexual relations before circumcision, the word would spread that she was a 'bad' girl and she would be denied the 'rite of passage'. Similarly, if a boy had been indulging with girls before circumcision he too could be denied 'the rite' and it would be known that he had been misbehaving. Before they went for circumcision they had to perform a purification ceremony and confess to the medicine man or *Mundumogo* all of their ill-doings. The medicine man would then put water on banana leaves and mix sheep dung and other medicine, a slaughtered sheep's fat, leaves of a sweet-smelling plant *mahoroha*, leaves of a creeper *mararia*, and dip all of this in water and put it in the candidate's mouth. Koinange remembered this being done to him.

'The *Mundumugo* held the potion over my head and then stuck the bundles in my mouth. After gurgling the mixture for several minutes, I then spat it out and in this way cast out all evil that was inside.'[7]

Irua: the circumcision ceremony. Testimony recorded by Ralph J. Bunche Jr after special permission by local Gikuyu chiefs.

'The first day was devoted to "preparing the candidates"; dancing, singing and rites performed very solemnly by the elders. In my group there were about a half-dozen girls, looking very small and solemn, and a half-dozen boys. The girls came marching up to the market in small groups first, two or three to a group, escorted by a throng of female attendants. They were attired in short sweaters or dresses and many beads and bracelets and other ornaments.

'We sang and danced (blowing whistles as we danced), the gist of the song being that we were seeking the place where the circumcision would take place. We danced vigorously at the market place for some time. Finally, the group broke and raced through a field to the ceremonial compound. Inside the compound was an arch of green boughs from which dangled a bunch of green leaves alleged to have been taken from the sea. It's under this square arch that the candidates would march into the compound, squat on the ground and meet the elders.

'There was a lot of dancing – consisting of jumping up and down outside the arch. Then larger girls, in attendance on the candidates, hoisted them on their shoulders and carried them under the arch and into the compound. Here we joined in the dancing, after which all candidates were lined up before the elders and "treated". Bands were tied about our ankles, twigs covered with a black-looking concoction called *dawa* were waved over our heads, and we were made to eat a nasty-looking greyish-black substance that had been prepared by the elders. There was more dancing and we moved on to another compound. Suddenly we all broke free and ran pell-mell across the fields and into a valley in search of the sacred *mugumo* tree, from which leaves must be taken for us to sit on when the circumcision takes place.

'We were given twigs of *mugumo* and after more dancing started back returning to the first compound. En route, groups of young women formed private dancing parties and sang all sorts of obscene songs about sleeping with men, and so on. We got back to the compound and were lined up one behind the other. We took turns at pounding sugar cane in hollow log pestles for beer or *johi*. We all had our heads shaved, except for one small round tuft of short hair at the top rear of the head.

'Finally we were marched in underneath the portal. Many of them were quite lit up with *johi* by this time, and there was some rather frenzied dancing going on. The men and boys whose duty it was to make room for the dancers were getting particularly violent with their grass whips and reed sticks, and were actually hitting one another, whereas before they were merely menaced. Now the candidates were again lined up before the elders, with our heads bowed, and the elders proceeded to strip the head and face decorations from the girls. Their faces were covered with a whitish powder called "snow". We put long broad marks down our foreheads and cheeks as well as large white dots on our ankles and rear ends. Finally the elders took some fluid from horns into their mouths and walked along the line of candidates, spewing and spraying it over our bodies and into our faces. There was more dancing and then we were allowed to go home, thus ending the first day of the circumcision ceremony.

'Early the next morning the older women began the process of preparing us for the "immersion" or *gwithamba*.

The immersion serves as a double purpose; it cleanses us and the cold water serves as a mild local anaesthetic called *kugandia*.

'We were all stripped naked and rushed into the water, where we sat squatting: women threw water over us, while dancing up and down, singing and doing the "ox-start". We were kept in the water about fifteen minutes, then we were led out, lined up and marched naked up the hill.

'When we got back the girls entered the enclosure and danced around in a sort of follow-the-leader fashion. The boys were taken to one side and made to sit on a small bunch of *mugumo* leaves. We were the first to be "cut" by the male doctor called *Muruithia-wa-ihii* using a knife called *kahiu-ga-kuruithia*. This was a tedious process and, as can be imagined, a bloody and messy business. We sat immobile while the *Muruithia* hacked vigorously away. It was a gruesome sight to witness. The *Muruithia* would stand back, survey his work, and then kneel down and hack off a few more odd pieces here and there until he was satisfied with his handiwork on each boy and girl.

'At the same time the girls had all taken seats in front of their "sponsors" on bundles of leaves. Then the woman doctor or *Muruithia-wa-Irigu*, an old, haggish, witch-looking woman holding a Gikuyu razor or *rwenji* shaped like a putty-knife, went to work beginning at the right of the line and deftly hacking off the clitoris of each girl. A bright patch of red appeared immediately between the girls' legs while their "sponsors" held them tightly and pushed whistles into their mouths to suppress their cries.

'As soon as the last girl was "cut", the crowd surged forward and there was wild shouting and dancing. Us boys had by now disappeared, leaving our "remains" behind. The newly circumcised girls grabbed hold of whatever objects that were in sight and began running recklessly about, chasing older boys and girls who had been taunting them. Blood poured down their legs as they ran about beating their tormentors. No medicine of any kind was applied to them after the cutting, nor were they even wiped off.

'The boys and girls did not go home after this ritual but remained with the elders at the compound for eight days of "celebration", after which they were supposedly healed. During the first day of celebration a male goat was killed and the circumcised boys had to tie a piece of goatskin around their right wrists.

'The girls put the skin on their left wrists. At this time a male sheep was slaughtered and its contents put on a ground of leaves of the *mahoroga*, under an arch suspended by two log sticks. The boys and girls had to walk over this and "enter the village". Upon doing this, they were led into a hut built specially for them, called *githono*. This was to be their home for the next few days, and here they were to sleep together without having any sort of sexual relations.

'On the third day their heads were shaved and they were given caps; the boys' were made from banana fibre and the girls' from sheepskin. The boys were also given earrings made from the roots of a plant called *muchagachugu*. The girls, on the other hand, had earrings made of goatskin.

'On the fourth and fifth days the boys were sent out to hunt with bows and arrows, while the girls were sent to the fields or *shamba* to dig potatoes.

'On the sixth day, before going out to hunt again, both boys and girls went to the *makuyu* tree and extracted white juices from it. The boys smeared it on their foreheads and the girls applied it to their temples. Each group then went out to their respective duties of hunting and digging respectively. Upon returning, the boys were made to dance the *ndirii* and the girls the *gichukia* dance.

'The seventh day was spent hunting and cultivating depending on the candidates' grade. On this day we did not sleep in the *githono* but instead spent the night in the hut of the first wife of the elder. All the goats were removed from the hut and the boys and girls were made to sleep together on the floor. The following night we returned to the elder's.

'On the eighth day, we dispersed very early in the morning and were allowed to go home.

'I was the first from my father's house to be circumcised

as well as the first in my circumcision group. I didn't feel much pain during the actual process but felt much pain for the first few days thereafter. On the day I was circumcised, I had to take five small branches of the *mugumo* tree in my left hand and a long stick cut from the *muthakwa* tree. When I returned home the elders were waiting and they took the *mugumo* branches and I retained the stick for dancing during the night. The *mugumo* branches had to be stuck in the thatching on top of my mother's house. I was circumcised in a place called Wambe in the village of Gathecha by a man called *Muhia-wa-Kiiro*. My *riika* was known as *Kienjeku*.' (Circa 1896.)[8]

3

Searching for a Wife

A long time after his circumcision, Koinange's father arranged for him to marry his first wife. This meant arranging a bride-price and giving a collection of cattle, sheep, goats and *johi* to the girl's father. The village of Kihara-wa-Ngaria, right across the Riara River from Mbiyu's village, was suggested to him. Kihara was a wealthy man and clan leader who had eight wives and four daughters ready for marriage at that time.

Koinange and two of his *riika* arranged to meet Kihara's oldest daughter, Wambui, to see if she indeed was interested in marriage. Wambui received them in her mother's hut. As soon as the warriors entered, it was customary for the girl's mother to leave her hut and leave them alone. They spoke to Wambui and told her Koinange was interested in her as his wife. She in turn replied that it was up to her father to arrange this matter. This was the indication that she was willing to be married if the father consented. If she did not consent, she would have said that she was already engaged to another man or that she was not up to the standard of marriage. But if she were willing, she would leave it up to her father to decide. Furthermore, if she didn't want the marriage she might have said she had the bracelet of another man, a sign that she was engaged to someone else.

Koinange returned home, and it was now time to begin making *johi* before sending word for Kihara to come and drink with them. Kihara arrived soon after with his entourage of relatives, and during the beer-drinking ceremony was informed that one of Mbiyu's sons wanted to marry one of his daughters and he was asked to allow Mbiyu to pay the marriage price, to which he consented.

Instead of sending *johi* to Kihara's village, they sent cows, goats, sheep and rams. They went to Kihara's village and met his elder relatives as well as Wambui's mother and Kihara's other wives. Mbiyu opened up the discussion by saying that they had come to be told what the price was for Kihara's daughter. Before saying anything, Kihara took a drink from a small horn of *johi* to bless himself and passed it to his senior half-brother. No one else was permitted to drink at this stage.

Kihara then took another drink and this time offered the horn to Mbiyu, blessing himself first by bowing his head and spitting the contents on his chest (the significance being 'so that everything inside may be all well'). He then handed the gourd to Mbiyu and asked him what his purpose was for the visit. After sipping, Mbiyu handed the horn back to Kihara and told him that he had come to get seeds for planting *ugimbi* (a sort of grain from which the Gikuyu make gruel). Translation: 'We've come to ask your daughter to join our family.' Kihara handed the horn a second time to Mbiyu and told him that if he could manage, he was more than welcome to have his daughter. At this time Kihara and his relatives left the hut to discuss the marriage price, leaving Mbiyu and his people alone inside. They returned shortly thereafter with Kihara's oldest brother, carrying *muthakwa* leaves, hiding them under their garments. Each *muthakwa* leaf represented ten goats. Kihara walked up to Mbiyu, handed him a bunch of leaves and told him, 'This is *ruiga* (marriage price).'

Kihara's brother also handed Mbiyu a bunch of leaves, saying, 'This is *irio* (clan's food).' Other leaves handed over represented everything from bags to skin garments, Gikuyu swords and a grain storehouse, cultivating knives and drums of honey to make *johi*. In all, the entire marriage price included four head of cattle, 350 goats, five fat rams, one big *thenge* (goat) and a dozen drums of honey.

Then came time to seal the partnership. Seated on stools, Kihara then mixed all the leaves together and held one end of the bunch in his hands and placed the other end in Mbiyu's hands. Holding the leaves in one hand and the *ugimbi* in the other, he then put them in his mouth. A little *johi* was then put in a calabash. This he drank but did not swallow any of it.

After gurgling the mixture for several minutes, he spat it out as a Gikuyu blessing to the 'seed'. He turned to Mbiyu and proclaimed, 'You now have the seed you came for. Let it be a blessing to you. Let the seed grow to be a great nation (many children) for you and yours.' Then he handed all the leaves to Wambui's mother, who took them and threw them down on the ground near where the goats slept. It was believed to be a blessing for the goats to trot all over the leaves. With this done, the ceremony was over and the celebration, which consisted of *johi*-drinking, began.

Less than a week later, Koinange returned to Kihara's village, accompanied by several young men from his village. They went to Wambui's mother's hut to eat and drink *uchoro* (gruel). He brought two necklaces made of iron with long chains in front, and took them to Wambui to wear – this is so that everyone would know that she was betrothed. But Wambui remained at her mother's home for nearly two years because soon after the bride price had been paid, there was a great famine in the area and it was deemed best to wait until after the famine before Koinange officially took Wambui as his wife.

The famine was very devastating for the people of Kikuyuland. Both of Wambui's parents died during this time from eating poisoned roots, collected in error, as there was no food. The effects of the famine were everywhere. In Kihara's family of over 50 people, everyone perished except three women, including Wambui, and a small boy. Mbiyu's family also suffered many casualties. Six of his wives, including Koinange's mother, were eventual victims of the devastating effects of the catastrophic famine.[1]

It can be noted here that it was mainly due to the devastating effects of the famine that (1) the Europeans upon coming to Kikuyuland, found very few inhabitants occupying land and therefore felt that the land was unoccupied and therefore a free-for-all; and (2) the Gikuyu offered very little in the form of resistance because they neither had the strength nor the numbers.

After the famine, Koinange brought Wambui to his stepmother's hut, where she remained for a year. He built a hut for her from fresh grass and timbers and did so in one day because she was his first wife. As soon as he brought her home he took her to an elder's hut in a nearby village, where a sacrifice called *hukoro* was performed, for which Koinange gave the elder a fattened ram for slaughter. This was because her father and mother had died and there had to be a purification sacrifice. It was after this that Wambui came to Koinange's stepmother's hut. Wambui remained in her new hut for four days and was not allowed to go outside.

She was also not allowed to work or cook during this period; these chores were performed by other women in the homestead. On the same day that Wambui became his wife, a fat ram was slaughtered and Koinange had to get a popular member of his age group to eat the meat found along the ram's spine. (This was meant as a sign that it's the first ram slaughtered to start one's married life, and the popular man should eat it to wish you well.) That night they had sexual intercourse for the first time.

Wambui later added the name Mariamu when she converted to Christianity. She had a total of 13 children, only seven of whom survived childhood. Koinange's second wife was called Julia Njeri, who belonged to the Muchera clan from Ruiru. She was related to the *Muruithia* who had circumcised Koinange. She bore Koinange six children. His third wife was Joyce Kagendo of the Anboi clan (the same as Mariamu). She also bore him six children, among them the author's father. His fourth wife he obtained by 'default'; before he married Julia Njeri, he had brought home another young woman and paid the bride price, but before he could go on with the marriage she suffered an illness and died. Her name was Wambui, and she too belonged to the same clan as his first and third wives. Since her relatives could not refund the marriage price to Koinange, they 'offered' him Wambui's younger half-sister, called Phyllis Wambui, in her place. Koinange knew she was too young to make such an important decision and decided that he'd wait until she was old enough to make the decision of whether to marry him or not. As expected, she married him, becoming his fourth wife. She bore him seven children.

His fifth wife was Elizabeth Gathoni-wa-Tharuba (the only one presently alive) of the Arimu clan. Her father was headman Tharuba of Thimbigwa, near Banana Hill, and she bore him seven children. His sixth wife was Beatrice Gataa, and probably because he married her at the height of the *Mau Mau* struggle (which we shall explore in detail in the coming chapters), she was only able to bear him one child.[2]

4

Forced Removal from Ancestral Home

Before the coming of the white man into Kikuyuland, the system of chiefs, senior chiefs, paramount chiefs and headmen never existed. There were elders who dealt with day-to-day tribal matters, but never chiefs, and certainly not government-appointed ones. There were what the Gikuyu called *Athamaki* or rulers, the most notable one being Waiyaki, but that was the pinnacle of the hierarchy.

When the *Lunatic Express*,[1] as the British-financed Uganda Railway was commonly known, made its way from Mombasa in the east towards Kisumu in the west, carving a destructive path through Gikuyu country under the control of the Smith Mackenzie Trading Company, surveyors were sent ahead to seek land that would be habitable for Europeans. Some of these surveyors were very convincing while at the same time the Africans, who were suffering untold losses from the devastating famine, were quick to accommodate any measure that would help to defeat the plague. Resistance was therefore practically non-existent.

The Europeans 'appointed' chiefs and put them in charge of various jurisdictions and gave them powers over vast areas of land. Land structure was divided into three main parts; crown lands, that is land officially owned by the 'British Government', land 'leased' to European farmers for periods of up to 99 years, even though no deals were officially signed, and land set aside for what was termed the 'native reserve'. It should be noted here that when the land was leased to settlers by the government, the natives who were on the land before were not recognised as owners of land. They became tenants at will of the crown. Those Africans who owned land previously now became squatters living on their own land. If the settlers wished to increase their crop output, all they had to do was evict the squatters at will. The chiefs' main duties were to provide a safe haven for the growing numbers of Europeans travelling through the area as well as providing suitable land for those who decided to stay.

One such chief was Kinyanjui, who was held with high regard among the Gikuyu until he fell victim to the ways of the settlers. Kinyanjui came to power after his predecessor, Paramount Chief Waiyaki, was deported upon defying an order from Francis Hall, an administration official appointed by the Smith Mackenzie Company.

While Waiyaki was chief, Kinyanjui was a headman and Mbiyu (Koinange's father) was an agent of the chief's. Some of Hall's people had been assaulted and killed by Waiyaki's aides after they went to collect a debt from him at Githiga near Kiambu. Hall demanded that Waiyaki pay him back immediately and the Paramount Chief, seeing his authority challenged, became so furious he drew his knife and threatened Hall.

As it turned out, Waiyaki was eventually overpowered, arrested and banished to a place called Nyamwezi near Mombasa at the coast. However, he never made it. Official reports say he died of dysentery, but many believe he was murdered along the way by agents of the Smith Mackenzie Company. Kinyanjui was next in line. He fell victim to greed and deceit. Since the great famine of the 1890s had wiped out more than half of the Gikuyu, much of the land in Kikuyuland lay unoccupied for long periods of time.

The European travellers, seeing such rich, fertile land seemingly unoccupied, convinced Chief Kinyanjui to allow Europeans to cultivate the 'unoccupied' lands and plant vegetables and other crops and help the people avoid another famine. Kinyanjui, without consulting the other elders on this very important issue, agreed. As the surveyors arrived to break ground for cultivation, the people looked on with curiosity at what they were doing and asked, 'What are these men doing and what are these lines (roads) they're making?'[2] But no one paid them any mind, as they felt the bush would grow back as soon as the Europeans left. But soon after, Kinyanjui brought several more Europeans into the area and also helped them build houses. The Europeans offered money to the owners of the lands 'for disturbance' (an offer made through Kinyanjui), but the owners refused. Kinyanjui, however, took and kept the money himself and the Europeans stayed on the land. The people did nothing about this as there was nothing they could do. Another incident, typical of what the early European attitude was like towards the Africans, was told by an eviction survivor.

> 'A European came to our place one day with Chief Kinyanjui. He had been told that he was free to settle on our land ... we were given seven days to leave. Seven days later the European returned on a horse and told us to remove all our belongings from our huts. He then burned our houses to the ground.'[3]

Koinange remembers that his father, Mbiyu, was chief, having succeeded Waiyaki, when the British arrived. He also remembers the chief swearing blood-brotherhood with the first administrator. The *mbari* never resisted the settlers, less because of friendly and trusting feelings towards the white men than because of the devastating effects of famine and smallpox in the area.

At about this time, the government, through interpreters, called together a *baraza* at Riara, and with all the chiefs present, the Provincial Commissioner asked the people of Kiambu to select a new leader. The people responded by saying they wanted Mbiyu to remain as their chief, but the PC insisted that Mbiyu was getting too old and the country needed a younger, more aggressive individual. The people unanimously responded: 'Then we will have his son, Koinange, as our chief.'[4] There was a resounding agreement to this and Koinange was appointed chief of the Kiambu area (circa 1905), with instructions to help white settlers coming into the area. There was only one European farmer in the district, and Koinange was told that many more farmers were coming and that he should help them take care of their property as well as provide labour wherever and whenever needed.

> 'Months later a meeting of chiefs was held in Nairobi, where we were told that there were too many chiefs and that many of us would have to be removed, and that those retained would be paid by the government. I was told that since I was on European land I must be paid by the European farmers and not by the government. This was the first time I realised the land belonged to Europeans and not to me.'[5]

One by one the Europeans continued to arrive. They were quick to occupy the land, tearing down banana trees and other crops to plant wheat and coffee. Initially, they never interacted with Koinange or his people. They just went about their business. One such method of taking over land began by the Europeans grazing their cattle along with locals like Koinange. When the land could no longer hold the strain of a double herd, Koinange would move his to a new pasture, leaving the European's cattle on the 'old patch'. The European would then fence this off and declare it his piece of land. No compensation was offered Koinange by the whites who settled their land. In other areas, however, some Africans were offered meagre compensation for their crops which had been destroyed.

> 'The Europeans came with good words, saying that they would come into the land, make it prosperous and because we were few in number, we did not at that time object, as we were thinking that all would be well, and trusting in the government. We soon found out that the Europeans who came as temporary occupiers, had turned themselves into owners, and us, the real owners, into tenants.'[6]

Koinange found himself in an increasingly precarious position as chief. On the one hand he was responsible for supplying labour for settlers wanting to clear land to grow their cash crops, and on the other hand he was collecting hut taxes from his own people, squatters now on land that was previously theirs. As Marshall Clough pointed out in his book, *Fighting Two Sides*.

'In the early years of British rule, the chiefs and retainers acted as the cutting edge of the administration, collecting hut taxes and labourers from their people at spearpoint, earning the hearty dislike of ordinary Gikuyu in the process. However, administrative reform, the revival of the *Kiama*, and the passage of time softened the brutal face of oppression, and the chieftaincy eventually came to be accepted – albeit grudgingly – by most Gikuyu. The chiefs became established in their own right, still dependent on their European superiors, but more and more autonomous in certain respects with their localities.'[7]

Successful chiefs became local institutions after periods of years, regulating the response of the people of their areas to the changes brought about by the Europeans. Clough goes on to say:

'Instrumental in winning popular acceptance for the chieftaincy (however partial) were men like Koinange, hard-working, progressive and concerned about popular opinion. It must be admitted that such chiefs were exceptional; the average chief was a fair administrator at best, showed little interest in innovation and maintained just enough popularity to keep his position. However, the better chiefs had an impact out of proportion to their numbers because official recognition brought them to the top of the chiefly hierarchy. The divisional chiefs were an impressive group, especially in Kiambu; and Koinange was the best of them all.'[8]

The relationship between Koinange and the encroaching settlers grew increasingly strained as the chief found himself giving in more and more to their demanding ways. Principal among this was the branding of cattle in order to separate the settlers' herds from the local ones. Once this was done, with cheap African labour of course. The next step was to fence off all European lands with barbed wire – more to keep unwanted herds out than settler herds in. All local labour was provided by the chiefs, as were the maintenance and upkeep of European lands. Other 'chief' duties included investigating settler cattle stolen by Africans, the appointment of headmen to ensure that settler needs were met, and of course the dreaded collection of taxes.

By the time war broke out in Europe in 1914, Koinange was surrounded by European farmers, all of whom were ploughing on what was once his land. The European farmers, being British first and settlers second, had to return and serve their various nations at the front lines. The protectorates also sent troops, in the form of Carrier Corps, to help uphold the empire. Two of Koinange's brothers served in the Carrier Corps and went to Europe to fight. They never returned, and no word was ever sent home as to what happened to them. No compensation was ever offered to the Africans who died at the front and whose military badge numbers were unknown. However, those whose numbers were known were paid wages for the duration of the period they served.[9]

World War I also had indirect repercussions on the Koinange family. Several of Koinange's European neighbours had to go off and serve, leaving the chief in charge of their cattle. Koinange's first-born son, Peter Mbiyu, was at this time already herding the family stock, and with the sudden increase the herd got too large and often strayed into the field of an unfriendly farmer. The farmer, finding the cattle on his land, seized all of Koinange's cattle, took them to the district headquarters and had them confiscated and locked up.

'I had to pay fifty rupees to the white farmer to get my cattle released. But soon after, they strayed over again and this time the white farmer demanded sixty rupees from me. I refused to pay and went to the *Boma* to complain to the District Commissioner, who ordered my cattle released but told me not to graze them on the farm any more but on the native reserve. I had to divide the herd in two because settler cattle were not supposed to graze with local cattle on reserve land due to fear of disease. I realised then that there was only one thing left to do in such a situation and so I decided to take my entire stock, family and relatives and move to Kiambaa. My father, Mbiyu, however refused to move with me, saying this was his ancestral land where he'd been born and where he would die and be buried no matter what.'[10]

On the morning Koinange moved his animals, the Europeans realised they had no herdsboy as young Peter Mbiyu had been 'relieved' of his duties. One of the Europeans rushed to Koinange's village with his labourers, carrying a gun, with the intention of seizing Koinange's property, but when they got there, the people were already tearing down the chief's huts, telling the attackers that Koinange had already left.

'I was sorry to move from my ancestral lands. We could do nothing when the whites moved on our lands, because we were afraid of being killed by them. We didn't say a word as some of our people had already been killed by the whites. We also believed that since we had refused compensation from the whites, the land remained our own.

'I came to Kiambaa and bought much land from the people. I paid fifty goats and five rams for one plot, sixty goats and six rams for another, and seventy goats and seven rams for yet another piece of land. According to Gikuyu custom, for each ten goats paid for land, one fat ram had to be given as well as one drum of honey, one ewe, a branding iron, an axe and a sword, when the transaction was completed. I also paid partly in cash, at the rate of twenty rupees for each goat. Some of the land I occupied without making any initial payment, agreeing to pay for it in installments.'[11]

At Kiambaa, Koinange decided to try his hand at growing coffee, since he didn't have as much land as before and coffee was a big money earner then. He went to the District Commissioner, G. A. S. Northcote, and asked him for permission to grow the crop. He consented and Koinange was able to purchase some coffee plants from his friend, Canon Harry Leakey, whose son, Louis B. Leakey, Koinange would later assist in compiling a history of the Gikuyu for a book he was working on. (The Leakey family allowed only 500 copies of *The Southern Kikuyu Before 1903* to be published. Today the book remains in high demand, but unfortunately can only be found in very few university libraries.)

'I also purchased coffee plants from European farms in Kiambu as well as coffee seeds, which I planted in a nursery. When they were about ready to fruit, one European farmer, Mr Knight, visited me and said he wanted to see my place. He spent the whole day here and saw all the coffee, saying: "Very good, very good," and went home.

'Four days later, Canon Leakey came and told me that they were discussing my coffee in Nairobi and all the Europeans were cursing him because he had given Africans coffee trees to plant, and they were very much annoyed by it and had resolved to come and pull down my coffee trees. Canon Leakey said he came because he was friendly with me, and he wanted to advise me to agree to pull down my coffee trees, and that I would be compensated for my trouble and expense by the government.

'He was sent to me by the meeting, and I questioned him: "What's wrong with my coffee trees?" Then he told me plainly that if I planted coffee, all Gikuyu will follow my example and the price of coffee will be reduced and the white farmer will lose money. The other reason is, he said, that the Africans will be stealing European coffee and no one will be able to check it because the Africans themselves will be raising it. He said we are not to be allowed to plant coffee and that if I did not agree, they will report the matter to the King in England and get an order from him to pull down your coffee trees, in which case you will get nothing.

'When I heard this I got rather nervous about it and thought I could not resist an order from the King, as I was not powerful enough. I was therefore forced to pull down my coffee trees after which Mr Knight came back with Canon Leakey and assessed my loss. I was paid one hundred and eighty rupees by the government for the coffee trees in my field. The coffee in the nursery was bought by an Italian farmer just below me for three hundred rupees and was planted right on my boundary. I've never planted any coffee since.'[12]

It should be noted here that just before World War I, African export production was estimated to be three times that of Europeans. This contributed to the government's decision, the result of great pressure from the settler community, not to allow Africans to grow coffee or other cash crops that would compete with European crops. The patent unfairness of this created more bitterness among Africans, especially among the Kikuyu, who were in the heart of the coffee area, than any other agricultural issue except land alienation.

Despite the obvious humiliation on his part, Koinange did not harbour bitter feelings towards the white establishment. But this did not mean that he'd forgotten what had happened to him and his family. Many years later he would complain to his friend and British Member of Parliament, Fenner Brockway:

'When someone steals your ox, it is killed and roasted and eaten. One can forget. When someone steals your land, especially if nearby, one can never forget. It is always there; its trees which were dear friends; its little streams. It is a bitter presence.'[13]

Koinange also took his complaint to Provincial Commissioner Northcote who, upon touring the land, told Koinange that his complaint was too little too late and it would be difficult for him to get his land back as the European living there had already built a costly stone house. This only fuelled Koinange's determination. He took his grievance a step further to the members of the 'Sir Morris Carter Commission', which had been sent by the Whitehall government to look into the affairs of the people of Kenya Colony and Protectorate.

In one particularly heated session, Koinange refused to back down from the intimidation of one of the settlers on his land, Abraham Block:

Block: 'I am considered one of the oldest practically in the upper Kiambu district. I came in 1902 or 1903. Koinange said that he was born in Njuno. I was the owner of Njuno, and I came and settled there. There were no natives there up to 1906 or 1907, and there was no Koinange in existence.'

Koinange: 'Did you find anybody living there? Do you know how many farms there are at Njuno?'

Block: 'I don't know how many there are now, but I know how many there were before.'

Koinange: 'When all these government officials came, I was living at Njuno. They found me there.'

Block: 'The whole of Njuno, which includes Kibubuti and Kamondo, belonged to me. I am called after that name by the natives. Originally a portion of Njuno belonged to Dr Ruffelle Scott, and the other portion was taken over by Mr Ross, who is in Canada.'

Koinange: 'I can still point out the graves of my grandfather and great-grandfather.'

Block: 'That is not true. There are no graves of Gikuyu. They were chucked out to the hyenas.'

Koinange: 'It was the Gikuyu custom long ago that when a wealthy man died they used to make a grave for him.'

Block: 'According to the native law, it depended entirely on the son if a grave were made or not. Where are the graves?'

Koinange: 'I can go there and show you. The graves I am referring to are on farm No 3562. There were *muhogo* trees very long ago, but they have all been rooted out. All these *muhogo* trees were finished or cut down by the children of Gikuyu.'

Block: 'Evidence can be produced that there were never any *muhogo* trees there, because the altitude is too high.'

Block: 'Do you remember when Kinyanjui came and made blood-brotherhood with me?'

Koinange: 'I was the headman, and Kinyanjui was living in my village.'

Block: 'I walked with Kinyanjui back to his kraal, and Marura was the chief at that time. Koinange was no chief at all. The Gikuyu custom is that if a man has only got one wife, he cannot be made a headman. He was not a headman at all, or even a sub-headman.'

Koinange: 'My father, Mbiyu, was chief, and when he died I took up the position. I was just like a *mnyapara*. It is not the custom of the country to go and live on another man's land unless one is a tenant. I moved from my own land during the Great War, and went to the place where I am now, and Canon Leakey can verify this. Before I shifted from where I used to live, Canon Leakey visited me. From 1902 to the Great War, I was living in the same spot I was born in. The old European travellers who came here, whose nicknames were *Nyanja* and *Dwara*, came to my father's village, and they took oath there with my father for peace and to help them, and Chief Mukoma was present.'

Block: 'Do you know if this claim of Koinange's is a new or old claim? I only heard about it a couple of weeks ago.'

Koinange: 'Letters can be produced which are in the possession of the government that I claimed this land in the time of Mr Dundas who was the District Commissioner at Kiambu. When Mr Block first came to his *shamba*, I had three huts at Njuno, and I had three wives. That is thirty years ago. I had about thirty head of cattle at that time, including calves.'

Block: 'Mr Hope came out to my farm when I was there in 1902 or 1903 to see what natives were there. I found six huts there and paid two rupees per hut as compensation. There were no cattle. I had to use tinned milk.'

Koinange: 'Each man herded his own cattle. We had many head of cattle before the great famine. Captain Lugard would say that it's true the Kikuyu had many cattle, but Mr Block only came after the great famine so he would not know.'

This exchange went on and on until the chairman, J. D. McKean, took Koinange's earlier suggestion of physically going out and seeing for themselves who was indeed telling the truth. Upon their return, the commission continued its inquiry.

McKean: 'Quite apart from the fact that whether Koinange was there or not there, there is a confusion in the mind of Mr Block about Njuno, and also in the mind of Koinange. To begin with, there is the *Mbari-ya-Njuno*. The *Mbari* claims a large block of land which includes the Njuno Estate and other estates. This morning, Koinange said he was at Njuno Estate, but he was on land which is claimed by the *Mbari-ya-Njuno*.

'We first went down to see the two trees where Mr Block says Koinange lived when he arrived first. Koinange then denied it again, and said he had never lived there. That is on part of Kibubuti Estate, and is not the land of *Mbari-ya-Njuno*, but is claimed by the *Mbari-ya-Thumbi*. We were eventually taken onto a *shamba* which I am told belonged to Major Borroughs, and which originally belonged to Mr Krieger. That is where Koinange says he was born, and his father and grandfather, and that their land stretched right down to the end of the Njuno Estate, but that they themselves were not actually living on it, and also part of Kibubuti Estate, but not the part where Mr Block says Koinange was living when he arrived first.

'We were shown places this morning where Koinange's father and grandfather were supposed to have lived and where they were both buried, and Koinange showed us where he had been ever since he was born, and that was on Major Burroughs' estate. Koinange is definite that that part of Kibubuti Estate, which was pointed out by Mr Block as the place where Koinange lived, belongs to another *Mbari*, and not the *Mbari-ya-Njuno*.'

Block: 'Koinange never lived there; he only came there. He was simply a stranger.'
Bell (Prosecutor): 'Did you see any graves?'
Block: 'I never came across any.'
McKean: 'We simply saw places where they had said a man had been buried.'
Block: 'I believe there are no graves there.'

Koinange: 'If you will allow me, I will go and dig up these graves, and produce the bones.'

The meeting broke up at this point, but a week later the following report was submitted to the commissioners:

'Under cover of his LND/2/VOL IV of 28 February, 1933, the District Commissioner, Kiambu, forwarded to the Commission a letter addressed to him by Canon Leakey, in which the following facts are stated:
 'Canon Leakey conducted an exhumation of the remains of the grandfather of Chief Koinange, whose name was Gathecha-wa-Gikonyo. The place was in uncleared bush on the lower side of a road made by a European settler to go down to his coffee factory on Riara River. There is a large coffee plantation on the upper, or left-hand side of the road. The place was pointed out to Canon Leakey by an old woman, a cousin of Chief Koinange, and the skeleton was found lying on its right side, with the knees bent up towards the chin, in an attitude which had been previously described to him. The skull and bones, which were nearly pulverised, were reverently removed to a coffin provided by Chief Koinange.
 'The site of another grave, said to be that of Chief Koinange's great-grandmother, was also pointed out to Canon Leakey, who distinctly saw that a considerable mound had been nearly flattened with a plough by the cultivator. No exhumation was conducted in this case.'[14]

This unforgettable grievance which was resolved by Koinange would draw him into protest politics after World War I, and the failure of the government to restore only a tiny portion of his *Mbari*'s lands (only 253 out of over 2000 acres) would eventually drive him into militant opposition to British rule. He would later vent his feelings to visiting American scholar and future Nobel Prize Laureate, Ralph J. Bunche Jr, who spent several months at Koinange's home while working on his Doctorate Degree in African Studies:

'I am not against any stranger; my father followed this custom and was always willing to receive strangers and help them as much as he could. But we have a Gikuyu proverb which says: "The cunning man does not always like to keep company with another cunning man. He prefers sometimes to keep company with a fool." As the white people are very clever people, and the Gikuyu are less wise, what will follow is that when the Gikuyu have got wise (educated) sons, these sons will consider what deceits and cheatings their fathers have suffered from the whites. And this will lead to mistrust of the whites. If you are a parent and you eat your children's food, they will lose faith in you and will not trust you any more.'[15]

5

Politics of Participation

Before 1919 Koinange had taken little part in Gikuyu politics. In that year he assumed a major role in a conflict between Christian converts and pagan elders and chiefs over land rights and bias on the *kiama*. At a meeting at Kabete, arranged by Chief Native Commissioner John Ainsworth and Canon Harry Leakey, Koinange acted as spokesman for the Christians, much to the chagrin of the natives. The question of anti-Christian bias on the *kiama* was settled by placing four of the Christians on the court: Koinange and Josiah Njonjo-wa-Mugane to represent the converts of the Church Missionary Society (CMS), Philip Karanja James to represent the Church of Scotland Mission (CSM) converts, and Waruhiu-wa-Kungu to represent those of the Gospel Missionary Society (GMS) at Kambui. With his victory in this struggle and his elevation to the *kiama*, which he would eventually dominate, Koinange became a political – albeit a controversial – figure to reckon with in Kiambu. For the rural Gikuyu, the critical problem in the immediate post-war period was to secure their rights to the land they still possessed. It's not surprising that the location of the earliest political organisation directed toward this goal was southern Kiambu, where the Gikuyu had lost the most land to the settlers. In describing the formation of the Kikuyu Association, its Secretary Matthew Njoroge explained that it rose from an attempt by the government to alienate some of his own *mbari*'s land:

'There was always trouble at Kabete about our *mbari* land,

which bordered on the Mission School ... in 1919 Captain W. H. Wood told the government he needed more land and, to our horror, they started to mark it out... Canon Harry Leakey suggested we write a letter to the government... we wrote the letter and it seemed that they listened since the land was not taken and we thought that this was a powerful thing.'[1]

With this success, the members of the Kikuyu Association realised they could have a strong ally in the governor and thought that if approached in a dignified and unified manner, he might just consider giving back to them their previously confiscated lands. According to Thuku,

'In 1919 we were invited to Kinyanjui's home along with many people from all over Southern Kiambu, including Philip Karanja James, Josiah Njonjo-wa-Mugane and the great Patriot, Koinange ... I became the first secretary of the Kikuyu Association, but because I was working in Nairobi, Philip Karanja James took my place. Kinyanjui became a kind of Patron and Koinange became Chairman.'[2]

Between 1919 and 1921, the Kikuyu Association engaged in a sporadic correspondence with the government concerning the Gikuyu lands. The KA requested a survey of farms in Kiambu and the issuing of title deeds to landholders in order to guarantee the security of the Gikuyu *Ithaka*. The government was reluctant to take these steps, pleading expense and lack of personnel and denying that individual landholding as such existed in the traditional Gikuyu system.

By 1921 the concerns of the KA had gone well beyond the expression of the land grievance alone. Koinange, Philip Karanja James and a number of others, assisted by Reverend Barlow of the CSM, began working on a comprehensive memorandum of grievances to be presented to the government, dealing with the demand for title deeds, the forced labour of women, registration, taxes and wages. The government agreed to hear the memorandum, and a meeting was arranged for 24 June at Dagoretti near

Kinyanjui's home. A number of Gikuyu from Nairobi attended the Dagoretti meeting, including Harry Thuku, leader of the recently founded Young Kikuyu Association. Koinange had become acquainted with Thuku during his visits to Nairobi and the two had often discussed the land issue.

At Dagoretti Koinange advised Kinyanjui to appoint Thuku to read the petition because his English was better than Philip Karanja James'. It was a move that would later prove fatal for the Association. Thuku knew the petition would have to go through the normal channels of communication, from the DC Kiambu to the Chief Native Commissioner to the Chief Secretary of Government before eventually being telegraphed to the Colonial Office in London. He also knew that along the way, the petition would either be diluted considerably or would eventually be conveniently 'lost' in the bureaucratic morass that was Government House. Instead he, along with several other like minded individuals, decided to alter the wording of the petition, making it among other things, inclusive of other tribes and changing the name of the organisation to the East African Association (EAA) with himself as chairman. Among the grievances in the new petition included the issues of labour, taxation, education and the issue of Indians. Also agreed at the meeting was to bypass the local administration and send the appeal directly to London. With that done, a copy was then sent to the local government, but it arrived shortly after London had already sent an angry rebuke to the Kenya Government inquiring about this insolent and unprecedented breach of procedure.

Thuku's actions led to a decisive split between the Kikuyu Association and the East African Association. As one member of the KA recalls:

'When Harry left with the Memorandum, Koinange and Kinyanjui were very angry ... that is why Koinange hated Harry's Association because of what Harry did at that meeting.'[3]

For the next eight months Thuku and the leaders of the Kikuyu Association engaged in an increasingly bitter struggle. As Thuku made his way through Kikuyu country, the chiefs would closely follow in his path, trying to counter his destructive arguments. At Ngenda on 26 January 1922, Thuku and the chiefs met in confrontation. Thuku boasted of helping *githaka* owners, stopping female labour, and working to end registration. He also became more and more contemptuous of the chiefs, telling his audiences:

> 'Chiefs are like dogs – they bark at the sound of other dogs, and when their masters want them to, and also when they want to be fed by the government. If I send a letter to the governor, any chief can be dismissed at once. You headmen are as nothing... You, Koinange, and you other headmen are as Judas Iscariot.'[4]

Following the Ngenda meeting the Kiambu chiefs submitted depositions to the government, asking that Thuku be stopped. They'd seen how destructive Thuku's Association was becoming and needed to put an end to it before things got completely out of hand.

On the evening of 14 March 1922, a squadron of police officers arrived at Thuku's house with a verbal order for him to accompany them to the Superintendent's office. Others with Thuku at the time including EM officials, George Mugekenyi, Abdulla Tairara and Daudi Waiganjo Ndotono vehemently objected to the order and instead demanded they return with a legitimate warrant if Thuku was indeed being placed under arrest. Thuku, however, realised the predicament he was in and decided to accompany the police lest they should need an excuse to use force to arrest him. Upon reaching the station he was placed under arrest and confined to a cell in the back.

Meanwhile word of Thuku's arrest spread like wild fire and before long crowds had gathered outside the jailhouse demanding his immediate release. Police reinforcements were brought in and a standoff ensued. This continued throughout the night and into the next day as Thuku's supporters continued to increase in numbers with some estimates putting it at close to three thousand. One of them was a certain Mary Wanjiru, an elderly fruit seller and unofficial group leader. She, along with several women went as far as to perform what was and is still considered the ultimate Gikuyu insult. In a defiant mode, they raised their dresses exposing their genitalia and breasts and continued to taunt the nervous white officers in front of them. Incidentally, across the street at the Lord Delamare restaurant, part of the very colonial Norfolk Hotel, patrons had gathered, some of them sipping tea and obviously enjoying the spectacle before them. Others though were armed and ready for any signs of trouble. With Thuku still inside and no one volunteering any information as to his status, the restless crowd surged forward aided by the ululating, naked old women. No one knows what precipitated the next move but some say a rock was thrown from somewhere in the crowd, hitting the leading Sergeant squarely on the nose. What happened next would go down in Kenyan history as one of the early signs of resistance to colonial rule. An order was issued and the entire police line opened fire on the surging crowd. At the Norfolk Hotel behind them another order to fire was issued and the helpless Africans were mowed down like dominos. By the time it was over, more than 125 Africans lay dead and hundreds more injured in the resulting stampede. Among the dead were the naked old women, who'd used the defiance as their last stand against this colonial oppression. But if anything the Europeans had succeeded in one thing, namely the disbanding of the East African Association.

These events, while destroying the East African Association as a functioning body, also seriously weakened the Kikuyu Association. The attacks of Thuku on Koinange and the KA and the response the chiefs decided to elicit had called into question the popular base of the organisation, whose efforts on the people's behalf had been overshadowed by the success of the EAA. Under the circumstances, it is not surprising that Koinange and the other leaders of the Kikuyu Association harboured a strong feeling of grievance against Harry Thuku. In Josiah Njonjo-wa-Mugane's words:

'We were fighting for one thing, the same thing. We were fighting two sides. But Thuku was interfering, saying chiefs were for the government. This was not true, because some of the chiefs were very very strong in fighting for their peoples' land.'[5]

The Kikuyu Association was a different group after 1922, primarily because the split with the East African Association and the involvement of the KA in the arrest of Thuku had led to the estrangement of many members of the moderate organisation. The number of decision makers dwindled, and the KA came to be increasingly associated with the Native Authority system in Kiambu.

The attitude of the government towards the Kikuyu Association was ambivalent but, due to its close association with the missionaries (J. W. Arthur of the Church Missionary Society, A. R. Barlow of the Church of Scotland Mission, W. P. Knapp of the Gospel Mission Society and the Canon, Harry Leakey), the organisation was somewhat protected from the worst effects of official suspicion. Although the missionaries continued to play the role of advisor to the KA as well as expressing legitimate concerns, their fervor for reform had been considerably dispirited by Thuku. They acted to suppress these moderates from expressing themselves too vigorously, afraid of another rising of popular feeling and, more importantly, of the government's response. But the organisation continued to send petition after petition of grievance to the government, meet privately with British officials, hold public protest gatherings and testify as a group before two parliamentary commissions, the Ormsby-Gore Commission in 1924 and the Hilton Young Commission in 1928. Its primary concern remained, above all else, the protection of the Gikuyu lands.

Official inaction shook the trust of Koinange and the KA in the good faith of the local administration. The arrival of the East African Commission, also called the Ormsby-Gore Commission, gave them an opportunity to go over the heads of the Kenya Government in a constitutional way.

The commission visited, among other places, Kiambu, meeting with chiefs and elders at Dagoretti to hear their testimony on the social situation in the district. Here, Koinange and the other chiefs saw their opportunity to put the government on the spot. Their testimony was highly critical of the administration, attacking official disinterest, inconsistency, and failure to protect Gikuyu land from settler encroachment. Koinange mentioned in particular the evil of evictions without recourse in law and drew attention to the plight of the landless. As expected, the Chief Native Commissioner and the Senior Commissioner both tried to contradict and refute this scathing attack on the government, but were not successful in deterring the chiefs. But all in all, African hopes raised by touring commissions were never fulfilled, although the presentation of petitions and testimony to parliamentary bodies remained an important outlet of expression for the Kikuyu Association.

After 1925, the KA in Kiambu had access to the Local Native Council, in which they could express their opinions on policy and had some role in making decisions that would affect their people. Here, Koinange saw an opportunity to pursue something he'd been wanting to start but was unable to. As early as 1926, Koinange and the Kiambu LNC discussed the possibility of establishing a secondary school in Kiambu district. His argument was that the only other high school in the area was the recently established Alliance High School, which had very limited positions for the many Africans who had come so far. Koinange presented his argument well, undaunted by the fact that his opponents were the very same missionaries who acted as advisers of the Kikuyu Association.

Finally, a mission high school was agreed upon and the money was approved but, four years later they were still waiting for the foundations to be laid, as the central government had opposed the spending of money. Once again Koinange and the chiefs were reminded of just who was in charge. Their shortcomings, despite genuine sincerity, were another display of not only the limitations of the LNC but also of the betrayal of their trust by the administration.

Koinange's high hopes for the LNC had come to little. Despite their active participation, the KA constantly seemed to be 'swimming against the tide'. Marshall Clough points out another of Koinange's shortcomings in *Fighting Two Sides*:

'As president, Koinange was often at a disadvantage because he neither spoke nor wrote English; by necessity he worked very closely with the secretary, Philip Karanja James, who drafted the petitions and conducted the correspondence. Nevertheless, Koinange was the real leader of the group, because only he had the prestige with the administration and popularity to win with the people and to win the association the attention it needed. The Kikuyu Association was more often than not referred to as *Kiama gia Koinange*.[6]

In his capacity as president, Koinange travelled all over the three Gikuyu districts to make contact with chiefs and headmen, visiting them in their locations or inviting them to meetings at his home at Banana Hill to discuss a common front to protect and recover their lands. Although he failed in his efforts to expand the Kikuyu Association beyond Kiambu, it was not for want of trying. He still believed in gradual constitutional reform guided by leaders like himself, rather than the 'politics of mass destruction' emanating from camps like Harry Thuku's.

At the same time, the violence and trauma of the Thuku affair temporarily discouraged political activity in the Nairobi area, though political discussions had continued in somewhat desultory fashion, mainly among African leaders from what is present-day Muranga, then Fort Hall. It was there in 1924 that a new organisation was born out of the old ideologies of the East African Association. According to its first president, Joseph Kangethe:

'We created the name KCA, which meant the Central Kikuyu Association, since we were all from central District of Muranga, and we made its house at Kihumbu in Kahuhia.'[7]

Even though Kangethe was the official head of the association, it was common knowledge that the real leader was the imprisoned Harry Thuku. A year later, Kangethe and another KCA leader, John Mbuthia, were accepted into the Fort Hall Local Native Council, the equivalent of the Kiambu LNC of which Koinange was a member. The two KCA leaders were so impressed with the oath of allegiance to the Crown during one of its ceremonies that they decided to incorporate their own version of the oath when initiating new members to the KCA. While a Bible was held up in the left hand, a handful of earth in the right hand was pressed to the navel, and the member swore to serve his people faithfully and to look after their money should he be entrusted with it.

At first, the administration handled the KCA with kid gloves. It did not quite know how to respond but, at the same time, anticipated an opportune moment to strike down any 'threatening' moves or proposed measures, just as it had effectively done with the Kiambu LNC. The administration did notice, however, that KCA recruitment was steadily growing. As the District Commissioner in Fort Hall was to later write:

'It can no longer be said that the Central Kikuyu Association is unrepresentative of the Kikuyu people. It includes in its ranks a vast proportion of the more enlightened and progressive youth, and yields an increasing influence on the counsel of elders.'[8]

One of these so-called 'enlightened and progressive youth' who would soon be recruited was a certain Johnstone Kamau, a water meter reader who'd been educated by the Church of Scotland missionaries at Thogoto, and who was to later change his name to the more familiar Jomo Kenyatta. This particular recruitment was to have profound effect later. At this point, it represented a crossover of the KCA, which had by then moved its headquarters to Nairobi in order to include Gikuyus from Kiambu. This immediately gave the Association a new and different dimension, as well as an injection of new blood.

Another advantage that Johnstone brought with him was his grasp of the English language, which was better than average, having been an interpreter for the local Supreme Court. The

Association slightly altered its name to accommodate this new move; it then became known as the Kikuyu Central Association and no longer the Central Kikuyu Association.

Among its earliest achievements and one which set it apart from the KA and other organisations was the creation of the first ever newspaper or journal by Kenyan Africans called *Muigwithania* ('He, who brings together' or 'reconciler'), of which Johnstone was its first editor. The main objective of *Muigwithania*, apart from obviously encouraging the education of its readers, was the attempt to restore pride in being an African and, particularly, a Gikuyu. KCA's platform, like the other organisations, revolved primarily around land rights for the people. Since they were considerably younger and therefore more active than the Kikuyu Association, they came across as more convincing and less government-sponsored. It can also be noted that by this time most Africans had witnessed the so-called 'impotent' power of the chiefs and their inability to get over the ever-present administrative roadblock. KCA's leaders were also more educated than the non-English speaking chiefs, and could at the time relate to leaders like Harry Thuku (who was still imprisoned but also highly regarded), Johnstone Kamau (Kenyatta), James Beauttah, Thomas Bell Mwathi and Parmenas Mukeri.

The KCA, seeing their power and influence growing, decided to bypass the local administration and send a delegation to London to present their grievances directly to the British government. They thought this would at least guarantee that their message would not be distorted or misconstrued in any way, as had previously happened. They chose two leaders for this. Although James Beauttah was an obvious choice due to his command of the English language, he declined because of family responsibilities. The list went on and on until finally the KCA committee selected the ever-popular Kenyatta and Parmenas Mukeri, the Makerere University-educated (Uganda) teacher as its two representatives. The local government was none too pleased with the KCA at this point, and tried hard to dissuade them from going. Their argument was that the KCA would never be granted an audience in London since they didn't represent the needs of all Gikuyu. But the KCA had made its decision, and Kenyatta and Mukeri set sail on 17 February 1929.

In England the two were joined by several influential and outspoken critics of the British policy in East Africa, among them the Rev. C. F. Andrews, who had visited Kenya in the early 1920s, and William McGregor Ross, formerly Director of Public Works. Together, they fine-tuned the 'language' of the petition and presented it to the Colonial Office.

Suffice it to say, the meeting with the Secretary of State never took place, but the delegation did get an audience with the Governor of Kenya Colony, Sir Edward Grigg, who happened to be in London on business at the time. Among other things the KCA asked for the release of Harry Thuku from detention, as well as the demand that Africans be allowed to own land and secure this through title deeds. Grigg replied that Thuku's release had already been discussed and that a formal date had yet to be agreed upon, and on the question of land ownership by Africans:

> 'The Kikuyu must learn to patiently argue their views out through local councils, a democratic process, which is going on at this moment in Britain.'[9]

Nine months later, Kenyatta was still awaiting an answer from the Colonial Office and a meeting with the Secretary of State. Parmenas Mukeri had returned home by then, but Kenyatta, still under KCA sponsorship, decided to do some travelling in and around Europe. He went to trade fairs in Moscow, conventions in Berlin, tours throughout France and Britain, all the while speaking out against the colonial government in Kenya. In an article in the *Sunday Worker*, a headline read: 'Give Back Our Land', in the article Kenyatta was quoted as saying:

> 'The present situation means that once again the natives of the colony are showing their determination not to submit to the outrageous tyranny which has been their lot since the British robbers stole their land. They have been denuded of their land and compelled by means of forced labour to work the vast natural wealth of their country for the profit of their

interloping imperialist bosses. Discontent has always been rife among the natives, and will be so until they govern themselves.'[10]

His article and others that followed must have had some effect because on 29 January 1930, Kenyatta was summoned to Whitehall to meet with the new Under-Secretary of State, Dr Drummond Shiels. Over tea and biscuits, Kenyatta sat down with Shiels and outlined his agenda and what his people were so desperately afraid was happening to them. The two discussed everything from land rights to education to the dreaded system of *Kipande* (registration), which many Africans were openly opposed to. Shiels' overall reaction to Kenyatta was guarded, and the only advice he offered him was in education:

'Unless you have an educated people to deal with, you may have the misfortune to put into force influences that you cannot control, and grave disaster to all your hopes may result.'[11]

Not much more was discussed, but Kenyatta must have felt that he'd been successful in relaying the KCA's grievances. He returned home in October of the same year to find a major crisis in Kikuyuland that was about to split the tribe literally down the middle.

6

Taking a Stand

Among the Gikuyu, as with certain other African tribes, the circumcision of girls as well as boys formed an important part of the initiation rites associated with *riika* (age mates) and entry into full membership of the tribal community. It was the outward symbol of a girl's reaching the end of her education and marked her readiness to indulge in sexual activities. It entitled her to a marriage settlement and consequent negotiations over goats and land for the benefit of her parents. All in all, the long-term rights of inheritance depended on the rites of circumcision.

For girls, the 'operation' itself involved the cutting away of the tissue surrounding the entrance to the vagina, in essence, the removal of the clitoris, parts of the labia majora and labia minora. The important thing during the operation was for the girl to show no sign of fear or pain, despite the absence of anaesthetics. Older women attended the ceremony and watched intently as each girl in turn was operated on, and they openly praised the bravery of those who were 'cut' and did not flinch. The circumcision of both men and women was part initiatory, part sacrificial, part sanctification and to a degree (at least it was believed) tied to fertility and reproduction. In so far as sexuality lies close to the centre of the human persona, it can no doubt be said that everything connected with female circumcision had enormous implications in the life of the community.

Perhaps Jeremy Murray-Brown best tries to explain the *irua* when he writes:

'The most plausible anthropological explanation of the significance of both male and female circumcision is that it inculcated a strong sense of corporate identity, and so was more deeply felt than mere initiation, but exercised, rather, a mystical hold over the people of a religious nature. Through mutilation and blood-letting were invoked the blessings of the ancestral spirits; they gave the seal of blood brotherhood to fellow initiates in their early life and, as in the Jewish idea of a covenant with God, confirmed the tribe's sense of a divinely appointed destiny in the world.

'Thus circumcision bound the community together, both the living and the dead, in a solemn and irreversible act which mingled blood with earth and so united them in the source of all life, the soil of Kikuyuland. Socially, circumcision determined the *riika* of boys and so the whole structure of eldership within the tribe; for girls, it meant sisterhood with their fellow initiates and a sharing with the boys of the same age-grade, though this did not have the same importance in a woman's life as it did for men.'[1]

European medical opinion condemned female circumcision outright. Apart from the agony suffered by the girl, and the risk of infection from the crude instruments employed and the lack of adequate aftercare, when the wound healed it formed a hard scar tissue at the opening of the birth canal which often made childbirth difficult and dangerous, and in some cases led to the death of the child. There was also always the danger of other complications affecting the urinary system. But at the same time, there were defenders of the custom who pointed out that objections to it, mainly from missionaries, were based on a prudish attitude towards anything to do with sex and that the real ground for conflict lay much deeper.

In some respects the most revolutionary aspect of European contact with Africa lay in the Christian attitude towards women. The missionaries taught that wives and daughters were equal with men in the eyes of God and deserved love and respect as individuals. Only in this light could sense be made of the Bible's teaching about family life and the consequent insistence in

Christian communities on monogamy, chastity, and the emancipation of women from their servile role in the tribal economy.

The impact of these ideas was nothing short of profound. Christianity threatened to turn African society upside down, as it had done in Rome centuries before. The missionaries found their hardest task was to convert girls, but once they succeeded the possibility existed of Christian marriages between Africans. Only in this way, could a new native Church be born. (Incidentally, Koinange was never 'accepted' into the Church since he'd already broken one of their cardinal principles: polygamy. He did become a Christian, however, as did his wives, who were all baptised.)

The question of female circumcision was one consequence of this struggle over the status of women The Protestant Churches in Kikuyuland were adamant in their opposition. The Presbyterian Churches and some others introduced rules forbidding its practice or encouragement by Church members upon pain of Church discipline – which might mean suspension from fellowship or denial of Communion or a setting back in instruction. Roman Catholics, incidentally, were not concerned about it.

It should be noted that in Gikuyu custom, the circumcision of girls was considered their coming of age into womanhood. It went as far as the belief that an uncircumcised woman could not bear children. Not to be circumcised was to be debarred from developing the personality and attributes of womanhood and to be condemned to forever remain psychologically a *kirigo* or little girl. In Gikuyu eyes, an uncircumcised girl of marriage age was an object of derision, indeed almost of disgust. Far from being unnecessary, the operation symbolised the most important moment in a girl's life, and her bearing during the pain that accompanied it was a matter of great pride or shame to her family.

Administrative officers and settlers with direct experience of female circumcision opposed it. Government reports described it as 'horrible mutilation' and a 'horrible practice', one of a number of 'barbarous ordeals'. But government action in the form of legislation was deemed inappropriate on the grounds, apparently, of unenforceability. The government at first refused to take any action against the practice.

In fact, at the Conference of East African Governors in 1926 it was decided that as the custom 'was of very ancient origin', it must not be interfered with, and an attempt should be made instead to persuade tribes to abandon 'the more brutal forms of it and return to the more ancient and less brutal form'. It was believed that this 'less brutal form' consisted in the removal of the clitoris only, which to them 'would appear to be harmless'. To this end, most Local Native Councils were persuaded to pass resolutions 'whereby the operation may only be performed by skilled women authorised by the council, and no operator may remove more than the clitoris'.

As can be expected, this decision was met with much opposition. It came to a head on two different occasions, in Nyeri and Kiambu respectively. In March 1928, the question was brought up at a *Baraza* called by the government at Nyeri. The meeting was attended by both Paramount Chief Kinyanjui and Kenyatta, General Secretary of the KCA. The KCA announced their intention of contesting the forthcoming LNC election on a platform of preserving tribal customs, including the circumcision of girls. The CSM countered by holding a meeting the following month and announced a campaign against female circumcision in the district. They also agreed to sponsor a political association that was going to oppose the KCA consisting of what they referred to as 'very educated and sane men.' They called it the Progressive Kikuyu Party. According to its constitution:

'It can only hold meetings during the daytime; it also asks the government's permission to do so and invites local government officials to attend. It stands for the fullest progress of the Gikuyu people, educationally and otherwise. It affirms its desire for active co-operation with men of all races in promoting the progress of Kenya Colony in general and Kikuyu country in particular. It wishes to abolish all harmful customs such as the sexual mutilation of girls and to retain only such customs as are decent...'[2]

At the heart of the whole crisis was CSM's Rev J. W. Arthur. He was joined by GMS's W. P. Knapp and CMS's Canon Harry Leakey in a classic case of what-goes-around. At stake, they believed, was the whole question of Church discipline, a matter of principle no doubt.

The Church had passed certain laws and all members vowed to obey them in accepting Christian fellowship. To oppose those laws from within the Church was not only a matter of rebellion against the way the Church was being run, it was a question of spiritual deception. The Church went after everybody, from its rank and file membership to teachers to elders and chiefs – the stalwarts of traditions. Everyone was required to denounce the KCA and its acceptance of the 'brutal 'custom and at the same time, declare their loyalty to the Church. Of 50 elders and chiefs, 32 agreed at once, including Koinange and the KA.

Those who didn't were immediately suspended. Rev Arthur took his 'mission' a step further when, in August 1929, he wrote an article in the *East African Standard* newspaper, explaining his point of view condemning a sentence that had been given to two women for circumcising a GMS convert. The KCA reacted immediately. Its president, Joseph Kangethe, signed a circular letter to each of the 74 chiefs in the province, asking them to approve a mass meeting of the Gikuyu to get to the bottom of 'this nonsensical act'. He also sent a letter to both Rev Arthur and Knapp demanding:

> 'Missionaries have tried on many occasions to interfere with the tribal customs, and the question is asked whether circumcision, being the custom of the Gikuyu Christian, he is to be a heathen simply because he is a Gikuyu. If we are to choose between circumcision and God, we take circumcision.'[3]

In September, Rev Arthur began his tour of the Gikuyu country, demanding that Christians at the mission stations sign an agreement to abandon female circumcision. There, Koinange and his KA came in direct conflict with the KCA. The chiefs sided with the missions and worked tirelessly to bring the situation under control, at the same time earning the enmity of the anti-mission forces. Almost overnight, it seemed, a scurrilous dance song swept through the villages to add to the dismay of the missionaries. The song glorified the KCA while at the same time ridiculing and vilifying the chiefs, especially Koinange, for their weakness in the face of the missions. Some of the verses included phrases like:

> 'Elders Koinange and Waruhiu, when Johnstone Kenyatta comes, you will be given women's loin cloths and be forced to cook him his food. The governor is called a big man, but when Johnstone comes he will have his teeth extracted like a *Kavirondo* (Luo) because of all the lies he has told Europe.
> 'We Gikuyu are delighted that Johnstone Kenyatta has been made Governor of all Gikuyu by the Secretary of State. Praise elders of Kikuyu Central Association for sending Johnstone to Europe who is stronger than the governor of Kenya, for he defeats the Governor of Kenya.'[4]

Ironically, the very Kenyatta who was being exalted in his absence was at the same time drafting a letter to the KCA at the insistence of Secretary of State Shiels, and other British Members of Parliament, asking among other things:

> 'Exalt the Chiefs, for the country that has no chiefs is no country. And the Chiefs should try to exalt those whom they rule, so that the fame of the tribe be enhanced.'[5]

Kenyatta denied that KCA members were involved in intimidation and rowdiness, or that the Association as a matter of policy was in favour of female circumcision.

In the short run, the dispute cost the CSM at Kikuyu over 90 per cent of its communicants and about half at Kijabe. Rev Arthur's attitude had also rocked the foundations of the Alliance he had struggled so hard to create, and greatly strained relations between the government and the missions.

By the end of 1930, the KCA was essentially a limited organisation in Kiambu, but the reputation of the Kikuyu Association had sustained a blow from which it would never recover. Koinange found himself forced into a corner, losing much popularity because of his strong pro-mission position. He and others in the KA were considered the main enemy of the KCA, whose membership had tremendously increased in Kiambu as a result of the circumcision battle.[6]

Meanwhile, before leaving London, Kenyatta had discussed with William McGregor Ross the setting up of a Joint Select Committee of Parliament to allow African representatives in all three East African countries to personally take their grievances to London, sponsored by the government. In March 1931, the names of the Kenya native delegation were announced. The first was Ezekial Apindi, President of the Kavirondo Taxpayers Welfare Association. The second was James Mutua, a Kamba headman from Muputi Location in Machakos and, to represent the Gikuyu, Chief Koinange-wa-Mbiyu of Kiambu. According to the government, 'Koinange is the most widely respected Gikuyu leader and is often described as Kinyanjui's successor.'

But again the KCA objected. The Kikuyu Association, for obvious reasons, did not have an across-the-board appeal. KCA's new president, Jesse Kariuki, and Kenyatta among others requested permission for Harry Thuku to give evidence, saying that Koinange was 'too inadequate a spokesman for the Gikuyu.'[6] This was denied, the reason being that it was too soon after Thuku's release from prison. On his part, Koinange seemed unaffected by the criticism; he knew this was the one big chance he'd been waiting for and secretly revealed to a friend, 'When one prepares for a dance, he already knows he will perform.'[7]

The group set sail in late 1931, even while the KCA was busy raising funds to send their own representatives. They finally raised enough money and Kenyatta and Parmenas Githendu Mukerie set sail, but arrived too late to testify. It turns out the KCA's fears in the inadequacy of their spokesman were unfounded.

Meanwhile, Koinange and his colleagues arrived in London in the autumn of 1931 and were met at Victoria Station by their guide for the tour, S. H. Fazan. Canon Harry Leakey would act as interpreter since he was fluent in Gikuyu, having lived among them all his life. The chief recalled that despite the cold temperature, he did not like the military overcoats they'd been issued in Nairobi.

Upon arrival he laid it down on a nearby bench but someone saw it, picked it up and brought it back to him. Asked why he wasn't caring for his coat, Koinange said he didn't like it. The following morning they were taken to a coat shop after Koinange's complaints reached the attention of the Secretary of State. Koinange told Fazan and Canon Harry Leakey that coats like the ones they had been given were worn by porters in his country, and he did not want to be treated like a porter.[8]

There were also problems over accommodation. It was felt that normal guest-houses would be unsuitable as white women might not like to eat in the same rooms or sleep under the same roofs as Africans. Ironically, an international hostel was found in Sydenham which was run by a woman.

Since the delegation was fully sponsored by the colonial Administration, they were literally accorded the grand tour, much in contrast to that which would be given Kenyatta and Mukeri two weeks later. Koinange and company were taken to see the changing of the guard, the Mint and the Tower of London, where Koinange got 'lost' for several hours.

He'd wandered off to look for a bathroom and when he returned, his delegation was nowhere to be seen. He summoned a policeman who took him to a local station, and fortunately one of the constables knew a little Swahili (he'd spent some time in Kenya on military duty) and Koinange was able to tell him who he was and where he was staying. He also mentioned Fazan's name and a call was put through, and both Leakey and Fazan arrived shortly thereafter to find Koinange very much at home with the local 'Bobbies', who were bemused by, among other things, his large-holed ears.

They also visited hospitals, museums and factories; they had excursions to Portsmouth and Aldershot and were treated to a bombing display at Farnborough. They also spent a day at Oxford and there attended an FA Cup final at Wembley Stadium. They toured Windsor and caught sight of King George in his motorcade.

But the highlight of the tour was yet to come. As he gave evidence in the House of Lords, Koinange charmed everyone and detailed the grievances from which he, above everyone else, knew the Gikuyu suffered. Nevertheless, he was hardly the friendly witness before the committee that the government had hoped he'd be. He spoke out strongly for the restoration of the alienated lands, for greater investment in African education and for the inclusion of Africans in the Legislative Council. Koinange also attacked the hut tax, the registration ordinance and the expropriation of land in the Reserve. A bold headline in the *New York Times* of 29 April 1931 read:

'Tell British "Father" Natives are Victims of Oppression and Discrimination by Settlers.'

The article went on to say:

> 'Native chieftains who rule over ten million natives in East Africa stood in the splendour of the King's robing room in the House of Lords today and pleaded for closer friendship from their British overlords.
>
> 'Wearing European clothing and not at all overawed by the magnificence of their surroundings, the chiefs testified before the joint Parliamentary committee which is studying the problem of closer union between Kenya, Uganda and Tanganyika Colonies.
>
> 'Chief Koinange, senior chief of the great Kikuyu tribe, listened gravely to the welcoming speech by Lord Stanley of Alderley, chairman of the commission, and then replied in his native tongue, his words being translated.
>
> '"I think of the committee as my father," said Chief Koinange, "but my mother is the land in which I was born. If my father – the British Government – were to die, I would cry, but if my mother were to suffer, I would also cry. I want the committee, my father, to realise that its children are oppressed."
>
> 'Chief Koinange protested against the monthly wage of $3 paid to the Kenya natives and suggested that the natives

often broke laws merely because they did not know of their existence until they were punished. He appealed for more education, in both elementary and higher grades, and then added:

'"No child feels shy in asking for benefits from his father. We wish to live in peace with the English, but in recent times we have had trouble."

'A closer union of the three territories could only benefit the natives, according to Chief Koinange, if they were admitted to the Legislative Council.'[9]

The chief had spoken out fearlessly for his people, no doubt feeling that his position as a civil servant did not require him to support the government's position. Koinange and his colleagues had forcefully and impressively argued the Africans' case, dispelling all fears and doubts about his position when it came down to his people's needs. Kenyatta was to later admit to Koinange's son, Peter Mbiyu, that the KCA had acted foolishly and unjustly in their condemnation of the chief and that, if anything, 'We misunderstood the old man.'[10]

When they left to return to Kenya, Koinange told his London colleagues, 'We have planted a tree of friendship in England and now we are leaving you to water it.'[11]

The impact of Koinange's testimony did not sit well with the administration in Kenya which, in his absence, was trying desperately to dissolve the Kikuyu Association, saying that the chief could not 'serve two masters'. His priorities as chief, they insisted, were with the colonial administration and not with his Association. 'He tries to run with the hare and hunt with the hounds, and is not successful in either capacity.'[12]

Soon after Koinange returned to a triumphant welcome back home, he redirected his efforts toward closer union with the KCA. Somewhere along the line, he realised that the two associations were fighting a common enemy and the enemy was not themselves but the colonial administration. Certain events around this time aided in bringing the Kikuyu Association, which had now changed its name to the Loyal Kikuyu Patriots due to political pressures, together with the KCA.

In June 1932, the two KCA representatives, Kenyatta and Mukeri, were still in England, having decided to stay after their 'failed' mission to gain an audience with the Joint Select Committee. Meanwhile, back home, the KCA was itself going through some major changes. Harry Thuku, the 'spiritual' founder of the organisation, had been released from prison and was running for election as President of the Association. He was facing stiff competition from others, most noticeably among them Joseph Kangethe and Jesse Kariuki.

In the end, his popularity carried him over and Thuku became President of the KCA. But the troubles did not end there. Even before he'd been installed as their leader, Thuku had to face charges of misuse of funds from his fellow members, Kariuki in particular. Thuku sued for libel and the case went to the supreme, Court, where after a drawn-out and ugly battle it was finally thrown out on very suspicious grounds. A split had developed in the only Association that seemed to have a solid following. In the end, Thuku was forced to give in and quit, taking his loyal supporters with him and forming a new organisation which he called the Kikuyu Provincial Association. Over the following years, Thuku became increasingly pro-government in his dealings with the colonial authorities.

By contrast, the KCA reverted to small cells of disgruntled people without a true leader. This was about the time Koinange was returning from England where, incidentally, he and Canon Leakey had had a falling out due to something Leakey had misinterpreted to the Joint Select Committee. Apparently, Leakey had said that 'Kenya was entirely suitable as a white man's country',[13] a report that caused a furore within the KA in Kiambu.

So heated was the debate over Leakey's loyalties that it eventually led to a falling out between the KA and their missionary advisors. The incident also revealed deep feelings of mutual distrust, and contributed to the estrangement of the two groups. This was also about the time the KA became the Kikuyu Loyal Patriots, and it was evident that Koinange and his association were slowly drifting away from co-operation and more toward a stronger anti-European stand.

The results of the presentation of grievances to the Joint Select Committee led indirectly to the formation of various commissions to look closely into the land situation in Kenya and determine whether it was as serious as the Africans made it out to be. The creation of the Kenya Land Commission in the 1930s, otherwise known as the Sir Morris Carter Commission, was probably the single most important event of the early 1930s that would eventually convince the local African groups of where they really stood with the colonial administration.

The months leading to the establishment of the Kenya Land Commission were turbulent ones in Kiambu. There was a growing resentment on the part of both Africans and settlers, and the rate of incidents ranging from the uprooting of coffee trees, the maiming of cattle and trespass confrontation, were on the rise. The appointment of the Commission meant the huge task of gathering evidence from the various *mbari* in this twisted maze of African politics. The KCA and KLP decided it was time to join forces and fight the common enemy, namely the Colonial Government. In the words of KCA officer, Josephat Kamau, 'They came to know that we were fighting for our land and we came to know that they were fighting for their land. Why do we fight two sides?'[14]

And as easy as that, old grudges were buried in this common cause. Koinange was called upon by the Commission and spoke forcefully and eloquently not only for himself, since his family had been robbed of more than 2000 acres, but also for other *mbaris*. He recounted the sorry history of the land alienations, conveying eloquently the helplessness of his people in the face of European encroachment.

Other grievances included restrictions on the growing of coffee, the absence of good roads or railways in the Native Reserves, the low level of agricultural extension services, discrimination in education, marketing and employment. His testimony was candid and uncompromising in its defence of Kikuyu Land Claims. Koinange also acted as an interrogator, challenging questionable statements of several key witnesses on the basis of his knowledge and experience of land issues. (His interchange with the farmer A. L. Block, which led to the exhumation of his father's and grandfather's remains was a direct forerunner of these heated discussions.)

The chief proved to be a pillar of strength and was unmoved by the opposition which included powerful and influential settler farmers from what was popularly known as the 'White Highlands'. But despite Koinange's efforts, as well as those of the other *mbaris* in trying to drum up enough sentiment in the face of mounting land problems, the Kenya Land Commission report published in 1934 only managed to restore a fraction of the alienated lands. It provided compensation for some, and rejected most of the rest of the claims.

Again Koinange attacked the bill's provisions, demanding more land for the Native Reserve and less for the 'White Highlands'. His own claims on behalf of *Mbari-ya-Njunu* had been rejected for the most part, and as an added insult to injury only received ten per cent of his original land back.

As he was to later recount:

'If I were a government advisor and if they would accept my advice, I would ask them to do what the Bible teaches: "Love your neighbour as yourself", because if they had a mind to do that, they would be trusted by everybody. They would be regarded as the parents of the people. If you are a parent and you eat your children's food, they will lose faith in you and will not trust you any more. It's very difficult to convert Gikuyu hearts when they turn against anything or anyone.'[15]

7

Mbiyu Abroad

The 1930s saw the real foundation of an African nationalist movement in Kenya. The most probable reason for this is what Koinange had been trying to stress to his people all along, namely education. Now, for the first time, there was a growing number of educated young Africans with new ideas, who were not prepared to submit to the ways of their elders. After his forced removal from his ancestral lands, his humiliation at the hands of the colonial government and total lack of appreciation by his fellow tribesmen, Koinange was determined that somehow he would have to find a way to overcome these obstacles, namely through education. It may have also been Koinange's foresight at the creation of a dynasty and a 'continuation of the bloodline'. As he would later recount to his friend, Ralph J. Bunche Jr, during one of his many interviews:

> 'As the white people are very clever people and the Gikuyu are less wise, what will follow is that when the Gikuyu have got wise, educated sons, these sons will consider what deceits and cheating their fathers have suffered from the whites. And this will lead to mistrust of the whites.'[1]

Koinange therefore decided to practise what he preached, and in 1926, after a chance meeting with Earl Cromsack an American teacher on sabbatical in Africa, the chief was able to send his first-born son, Peter Mbiyu, to school in the United States. Naturally it was an extremely difficult adjustment for the son of a chief who, despite the fact that he'd gone to one of the best secondary schools in the county, the Alliance High School, he found that he now suddenly had to fend for himself in a land so far away and a people so different from his own. Mbiyu was in the unenviable position of pace-setter, and the pressure was on for him to 'come back with knowledge'.

He first attended Hampton Institute in the State of Virginia. But Hampton proved a difficult adjustment with its notoriously harsh winters. It was some time in the middle of his first semester that young Mbiyu contracted a serious case of tuberculosis. He was immediately admitted into the State Sanatorium for Negroes at Burkeville, Virginia, where he would remain for the better part of a year.

Since his was a rare case, having come from Africa, officials at Hampton were not sure how to handle the situation. But the Institute was one of the finest for blacks at the time (segregation was still very much in effect in the late 1920s), and Mbiyu very soon began to show signs of recovery. He was especially concerned that word of his illness should not reach his family in Kenya Colony. He particularly didn't want his father to be worried about his first-born son being gravely ill in hospital for so long instead of studying in school. In a letter to the Principal of Alliance High School in Kikuyu, Mbiyu's college dean Dr Phoenix had to finally break the news of the young man's illness:

> 'Peter Koinange asked us not to write, lest it should give undue alarm to his family. Now that he seems quite surely on the road to a full recovery, I think that I ought to tell you, confidentially, that he was taken with incipient tuberculosis last November, and was promptly removed from the institute to the State Sanatorium for Negroes at Burkeville, Virginia. There he has been, in the opinion of the Superintendent, the best patient that he has ever had, following directions with scrupulous conscientiousness, and making steady progress back to health and strength. He has gained about thirty pounds, has had to have new clothes sent to him because of this, writes cheerful letters,

and is now looking forward to returning to the institute next fall. We have reason to thank God that the boy's case was so promptly diagnosed and so competently handled at the Sanatorium. When he comes back to the institute, we shall, of course, watch him closely and see that he is relieved of physical work which would involve any undue strain.'[2]

Nearly a year later, he'd been re-admitted into the rigorous Hampton schedule and quickly proved himself, averaging a 'B' grade in his subjects. He also joined the Institute's soccer team and became an instant celebrity. He seemed to have many of his father's natural abilities of communication and, more so, had a huge appetite for learning. He also had a penchant for telling his fellow American students what his homeland was like and what sort of background he grew up in.

Naturally this raised a lot of interest to a student body which, at the time, knew very little or nothing about the 'dark continent'. In fact, at one of his many visits to the Hampton University Museum, Mbiyu noted that in the African section there was nothing that represented his homeland. After inquiring why this was so, he was told that no exhibits were available since they were so difficult to obtain. His college guidance counsellor recollects:

'Peter wrote his father and told him of the absence of African artefacts and asked what should be done about it. His father told him not to worry and sure enough, six months later, a container arrived filled with every conceivable item of the Kikuyu tribe, ranging from a chief's regalia made of genuine Colobus-monkey skin, to spears and arrows and shields and gourds and bags. It was an impressive collection of items, and Peter was all too happy and honoured to explain what each and every piece was used for.'[3]

To this day, there exists the 'Koinange Collection', at the Hampton University Museum, and encased in a glass container is the chief's regalia as well as many of the items that Chief Koinange shipped more than 70 years ago.

In Hampton's Senior Yearbook Class of 1931, Mbiyu was referred to by his classmates in the following words:

> 'A noble person goes on his way conscious of his nobility.'[4]

From Hampton, Mbiyu went on to Wesleyan University in Delaware, Ohio, where he continued to excel in his studies. He was also an excellent debater, and in his senior year was made President of the Political Science Club. He graduated in 1934 with a Bachelors of Science degree in Political Science, the first Kenyan ever to obtain a degree. But he wasn't satisfied with this. He applied and was accepted to the Teachers College of Columbia University in New York City, where he was exposed to much of what was happening during the great depression of the 1930s, more so than in the Midwest. But Mbiyu was determined and his perseverance won the better of him, graduating with honours as part of the Class of 1936.

From there he attempted to gain entrance into Yale to pursue a Doctorate, but was denied entry due to his early poor performance, despite written pleas from his professors and even the Institute's President. Yale's President at the time, Charles T. Loram, in a reply to Arthur Howe, President of Hampton, stated:

> 'I am inclined to think that Mr Peter Koinange should content himself with the MA degree from Columbia and should not attempt the PhD at Yale.'[5]

Needless to say, Mbiyu won a fellowship to study at St John's College, Cambridge University in England, where he would continue on his education binge. A year later he'd won a further fellowship at the University of London, Institute of Education. He arrived in England to find many more Africans than there were in the United States, but mostly from West Africa. Students then, but future leaders such as Kwame Nkrumah of Ghana, Milton Obote of Uganda and Yakubu Achiengpong of Nigeria, among others, were the many he would come in contact with during his stay there.

There was also a fellow Kenyan whom Mbiyu would meet before long, a meeting that would forever alter both of their lives. In the meantime, he'd heard that a certain American Doctoral student was about to embark on a trip to Africa and was seeking advice and guidance on how best to traverse the continent. The student was introduced to Mbiyu because he'd been to the United States and would be best able to advise him. It turned out that it was one of the wisest moves Ralph J. Bunche Jr would make in his life.

He and Mbiyu established a great rapport from the start and spent many afternoons picking each other's brains on issues and views that affected both their peoples on the two continents. They also discussed the adventure that was about to take place for the young American. Mbiyu gave Bunche his father's contact, saying that as soon as he got to Mombasa to cable the chief and the rest would be taken care of. Mbiyu also wrote to his father, telling him to expect a visitor who would be spending some time with the family while working on his Doctorate degree. On arrival at Mombasa, Bunche was understandably a little apprehensive, and all along the train ride to Nairobi didn't know what to expect.

It turned out that his anxiety was unnecessary: he was received like a long-lost son and ended up extending his stay in Kenya due to the hospitality accorded him. Moreover, he spent most of the time as a guest of Chief Koinange. And the Gikuyu people, seeing his light skin but distinct African features, gave him the nickname Karioki, meaning 'one who has come back from the dead'.[6]

They were more than convinced (and rightfully) that Bunche's ancestors had been stolen from this land and taken to a far away place and that now, many years later, he had returned and, in essence, 'risen from the dead'. He ended up spending several months in Kenya before travelling to Uganda and South Africa. Staying at Chief Koinange's he was exposed to the way of life of the Kikuyu, and in particular found the diminutive, humble chief a fascinating subject; so much so that he one day asked him if he would agree to be interviewed as part of a biography.

The chief heartily agreed, and the two spent weeks travelling from place to place, meeting various people of all races and backgrounds and, in between, Bunche wrote notes and experiences in his diary about his experiences. One such went like this:

Monday 31 January 1938:
'Chief Koinange's son-in-law picked me up from the train station and drove me to town. We passed by a record shop and since I'd heard the old man was a big music fan, I decided to pick up a couple of records. Ended up buying Paul Robeson, Jo Baker, Fats Waller and Benny Goodman for Chief Koinange's gramophone. Got my watch fixed and mailed a letter to (my wife) Ruth.

'The chief came out to greet us as we drove up. He offered me a choice of quarters – sleeping in a room in the "big" house or in the small guest house adjacent to the main house. I chose the latter.'

Thursday 3 February 1938:
'Had luncheon with five chiefs, Koinange, Josiah, Philipo, Muhoho, Waruhiu and an elder of the Kiambaa court.'

Tuesday 8 February 1938:
'We left at 8:30 a.m. for Githunguri Native Tribunal where the governor was to meet the Kiambu people. Got there at 9:30. Waited until 11:30 for the governor. Chief Waruhiu is scurrying all about, yelling at everyone, trying to get things in order. Chief Koinange didn't bother much. The governor made the sort of speech that would be expected, but Chief Koinange dug right into the many grievances of the natives in his reserve. Later in the evening I visited Peter Mbiyu's mother in her hut in the same compound as the chief. She received me very cordially. Everyone has already begun to greet me as "Karioki" [Kariuki] – he who has returned from the dead. It was real

cosy sitting before the fire in Peter's mother's hut, inhaling smoke and grinning – that's all I could do since I know only a dozen Kikuyu words.'

Friday 8 April 1938:
'With Stephano interpreting, I got to work on Koinange for his life story and made good progress. I keep hearing Robeson in the background singing "Old Man River", sounding very bizarre out here in the middle of the Native Reserve.'

Monday 22 April 1938:
'Had a Kikuyu dinner, fried bananas, sweet potatoes and was finally able to tie down the Chief so that we can finish off our interview session. He's such a fascinating man, so full of life and only wants the best for his people. He is in my opinion the true leader of this great tribe.'[7]

Bunche was to later write a paper published in the *Journal of Negro Studies* on 'The Land Equation In Kenya Colony', based on his experiences in Kenya and seen through the eyes of a Gikuyu chief. One of his excerpts reads:

'In the presentation of the grievances of the Kikuyu, Senior Chief Koinange of Kiambu district has played a prominent part. He is *Kikuyu Karinga* – pure and independent Kikuyu – proud of his people's past, well thought of by his subjects, and a man of noble qualities. He has been awarded several King's medals, but remains independent, and is more than qualified to speak for his people.'[8]

Bunche also spent time with the other leaders of the KCA and became very familiar with the customs of the Gikuyu. So close was his relationship with the chief and his people, Koinange even offered Bunche an incentive to stay in Kiambaa. Bunche always marvelled at how the chief's wives were so accommodating of each other and how well they divided their duties of taking care of their 'household'.

'Chief Koinange offered me a *shamba*, a hut, sheep and goats and 5 wives if I would stay. He even would permit me to bring my "first" wife over too. I told him it was a tempting offer because in my own country I had no *shamba*, no house, no animals and only one wife and I had to struggle to support her. That tickled him and his people immensely.'[9]

One of his greatest and most memorable highlights was when he was granted permission to take moving pictures of a Gikuyu circumcision ceremony, a privilege never before granted a foreigner. He used his cine camera and recorded hours and hours of what he later called 'The most horrific and barbaric scenes I've ever seen. But the most amazing thing is that no one is forced to partake. It's all a ritualistic occurrence.'[10]

Bunche was also able to travel extensively throughout East, Central and Southern Africa, including a visit to the Kabaka of Buganda as well as a brief stopover in Durban, South Africa, where he'd get to meet a young, progressive but fiery lawyer by the name of Nelson Mandela. His and Koinange's paths would indirectly cross much later, when he was Under-Secretary General of the United Nations. As we shall see later, he would apply pressure on the colonial government during the Emergency period to allow for the jailed Koinange to be granted early release from detention.

Peter Mbiyu, meanwhile, was still at Cambridge, where he continued his penchant for learning. He was now meeting more and more pan-Africanists who were yearning to return home to fight for their people's freedom. The Leakeys meanwhile had warned him against socialising with one Johnstone Kamau, known now by the more popular name, Kenyatta, and considered a radical and a 'bad influence' on others. They also said he was writing a book that was 'very unflattering' of the Gikuyu. Mbiyu would later find out that Leakey's jealousy of Kenyatta stemmed from the fact that Louis B. Leakey, the son of Canon Harry Leakey, with the help of Chief Koinange, was in the process of compiling a comprehensive three-volume anthropological study of the Gikuyu entitled *The Southern Kikuyu Before 1903*.

Mbiyu was briefly acquainted with Kenyatta but knew him more as the motorcycle-riding water-meter reader who dressed flamboyantly and wore a distinctive beaded belt (called a Kinyatta in Maasai). He'd also learnt that Kenyatta and the KCA had strongly opposed Chief Koinange's selection as one of the African Representatives to the Joint Select Committee and how such opposition had proved short-lived by the chief's evidence to the British Parliament in 1931. The two finally met in an anthropology class taught by the famous Branislav Malinowsky and, after a brief moment of uncertainty, discovered they had more in common and less to lose by being friends.

On Mbiyu's part, Kenyatta was a wealth of information, an enigma of sorts. He was a source of great conversation and intellectual stimulation both in and out of class:

'I wanted to catch up as much as possible with the new developments since I left Kenya in 1927. As a university graduate and with Kenyatta as a colleague at Professor Malinowski's seminar, I used to raise Kenya's question to an academic level. His five years' absence from Kenya and his experience in social anthropology had sharpened and mellowed his answers. He also explained, with a degree of restraint, how he got the mandate to oppose Chief Koinange and how such opposition had proved abortive, and quashed by the chief's evidence given to the Joint Parliamentary Committee.'[11]

Kenyatta would confess to Mbiyu:

'We misunderstood the old man. People thought that Koinange's lack of understanding of the English language and his position as government-appointed chief would hinder his effective stand for the Africans before the Committee.'[12]

Among other things Kenyatta explained to Mbiyu the differences between the Kikuyu Central Association and the Kikuyu Provincial Association, and also between the Kikuyu Patriotic groups to which chiefs and non-members of the Central and Provisional Associations got affiliated.

'We used to adjourn either to his room at Cambridge Street or to my place at Woburn Square and continue arguments until late at night. He spoke freely about his dormitory life at the Church of Scotland Mission School at Kikuyu, and I would return the compliment by describing my life in Harlem, New York; Hampton, Virginia; and in Delaware, Ohio. I'd also talk about the depression of the 1930s, about the New Deal, Jessie Owens, Joe Louis and many more. So far as we were concerned, Africans from Kenya or elsewhere were all Africans.'[13]

Murray-Brown perhaps put it best when he noted in his book, *Kenyatta*:

'With his intelligence and American experience, Mbiyu was stimulating company for Kenyatta. Mbiyu too was somewhat impressed with the flamboyant and flashy Kenyatta and his circle of left-wing friends, ranging from Ghana's Kwame Nkrumah to the West Indian Trade Unionist, George Padmore, and of course the famous American actor and close personal friend of Kenyatta, Paul Robeson.'[14]

Mbiyu was also very anxious to help Kenyatta in any way he could with a book he was working on, later entitled, *Facing Mount Kenya*.

'Jomo wore my hyrax and blue monkey cloak for a photograph to be used in the author's preface to his book, *Facing Mount Kenya*. We sharpened a piece of wooden plank for a spear. Our main object was to give the book on *Agikuyu* – by an elderly *Mugikuyu* – a more mature and elderly tone in contrast to books written by non-Africans about us. 'What others can do, we too can do,' we said. Let us therefore put the author in a proper elderly background. This was followed by the crossword puzzle to retain "J" in Johnston and the coining of an African name to go with Kenyatta. "Why all this trouble, man, don't you have a name?" I asked. He hesitated for a while, still with his pen on the paper. I repeated my question, but his thoughts were still centered on the puzzle before us. "My name is Kamau." "And your father's name," I interrupted. "Ngengi," he replied. "Then why on earth are we taking all this trouble to find names while you have "Kamau Wa Ngengi?" You see, I am known by the name Kenyatta, I want to retain it." We proceeded to make a combination of vowels and consonants until we agreed on "Jomo".'[15]

With his new name and a book soon to be on the market, Jomo Kenyatta was literally making a name for himself that would propel him onto the international stage as a force to be reckoned with. Much later during Kenyatta's trial at Kapenguria, the authorities would try to depict *Facing Mount Kenya* as a textbook for violence. The press described the wooden spear he is seen holding in a photograph as the 'Burning Spear'.

By 1938, Mbiyu had already spent a dozen years abroad and he felt it was time to go back home and take part in cementing a base for future political nation-building. Even though the two academic years in Britain had provided him with an opportunity to know Jomo better, his going back home was a testing period for the two. Kenyatta had no illusions about Mbiyu's better standing in the colonial world. He was the son of the senior and most respected Gikuyu chief, and he could now boast several university degrees and an English diploma. Mbiyu's future seemed bright, while Kenyatta was losing touch with not only his family but the KCA as well. Mbiyu's departure was a reminder to Kenyatta of his own lengthening separation and isolation. Mbiyu later recalled:

'When Jomo saw me off at Victoria Station, he made a personal request that I look after his family in Dagoretti. He said it with the fullest confidence derived from the experiences we had shared in London. I wanted him to come back so that we could continue serving our country and people with mutual understanding and respect.'[16]

Mbiyu's homecoming in 1938 was exciting news nationwide, especially for the African youth of Kenya. It was a renewed dream come true to see, for the first time, a university cap and gown worn by one of their own. Parents across Kenya set a new educational target for their children to 'be like Mbiyu.' A new dawn had arrived for African Independent Schools.

At a reception held in Mbiyu's honour at his father's home in Kiambaa, a committee selected from the chiefs, elders and representatives of Independent Schools asked Koinange to 'loan' them his son to train teachers for their schools. At the same time, the Administration, in trying to monitor his activities lest he become too outspoken, offered him a minor post in the educational department, but at a salary lower than less-qualified Europeans with poorer qualifications vying for the same position. As can be expected, Mbiyu declined the offer.

In the same year, Senior Chief Koinange brought together a number of age-groups to help raise funds to transform the Githunguri Kikuyu Independent Schools Association or KISA into a higher college not just for the Gikuyu but for all Kenya Africans. By this act, the second major feature of Gikuyu social structure, the *riika*, was harnessed into modern politics. At the meeting, Koinange announced to the representatives of the most senior age-group, *Njunge*, that 'this school will be the grinding stone on which we will sharpen our children.'[17]

The following January, the Kenya Teachers' College was established in Githunguri and Mbiyu was made its first president. This time he had the full support of his father, who was now leaning more and more towards militancy.

At about the same time, serious criticism of the chief began appearing in the local record. A report by the District Commissioner, Anderson, said:

'Koinange can no longer be considered reliable because of a conflict of interest between his loyalty to government and his feelings of responsibility toward his Gikuyu constituency.'[18]

In a classic case of the Machiavellian colonial strategy of divide and conquer, divide and rule, in 1941, after 45 years of local service to the government, Senior Chief Koinange was relieved of his duties as Senior Chief but he retained the position of Chief-without-location. He was replaced by a close friend of his, the younger loyalist and pro-government stooge, Waruhiu-wa-Kungu. As Marshall Clough writes:

> 'Koinange and Waruhiu had been friends for a long time, but the latter disapproved of Koinange's involvement in militant politics. Waruhiu may have also resented Koinange's elevation to Senior Chief in 1938. After Koinange was removed from his position as Senior Chief, Waruhiu was appointed in his place, and reports of bad relations between the two appeared in the official record.'[19]

This didn't seem to faze Koinange. He now had a new 'battle' to fight, and more so had the support of his fellow Gikuyu who now began to realise how wrong they'd been when they had questioned the chief's loyalties. He immediately threw his weight behind his son, Peter Mbiyu, in getting him elected as the first African representative to the Legislative Council. Mbiyu was eventually passed over by another young and promising leader, Eliud Mathu, a move seen as yet another slight against the Koinange family by the colonial Administration. Later on, when Mbiyu would depart to England once again to represent the growing nationalist movement abroad, Koinange would link up with two other sons, both from different wives, and another young man would become his son-in-law, to form his 'inner circle'. John Westley Mbiyu, otherwise known as 'the Senator' and the first-born of his second wife, would be his personal driver and most-trusted aide, and Frederick Mbiyu, first-born from his third wife, his personal assistant and secretary. Note the similarity in the names of all three sons, all having been named after the chief's father, Mbiyu.

Senior Chief Koinange (top left) with members of the Indian community in Nairobi 1943

'He was a diminutive man, barely 5 feet tall, but a giant in Kenya's political history.' At his home in Kiambaa, 1945

Senior Chief Waru Hiu lying dead in his Hudson car after he'd been shot 7 October 1952. Among those implicated in his murder were Senior Chief Koinange and his two sons, John Mbiu and Noah Karuga. They were tried but later released for lack of evidence

Senior Chief (2nd left) with other senior Kikuyu chiefs, 1947

Senior Chief with two of his wives, Mariamu (wife no. 1) and Julia Njeri (wife no. 2)

Outside his thingira (house) in traditional chief's clothing, Kiambaa, 1948

Senior Chief with Elizabeth Gathony (wife no. 5) and one of her seven children. She's his only surviving spouse

'Kikuyu Karinga' - Pure Kikuyu. The Senior Chief in his regalia, 1946

Senior Chief Koinange addresses a Baraza in Kiambu 1947. He was a diminutive man but when he spoke people listened

Senior Chief seen in a serious mood with his first born son, Peter Mbiyu

In a serious, contemplative mood, 1948

Senior Chief Koinange and Chief Josiah Njonjo

Posing after receiving his King's Cross medals, 1948

Protest Discrimination

A party of African chiefs leaving the Jewel House of The Tower of London in their tour of London, England. They are in the British capital to appear before the joint parliamentary committee on colonial relations protesting against the discrimination by British settlers and asking for a closer union of the territories which they (the kings) represent. Senior Chief Koinange is in the foreground (with cane) 1931

Photo by International Newsreel

House of Joyce Kagendo (wife no. 3) 1949. Frederick Mbiyu (author's father) is in the front row (seated), Joyce Kagendo is in the second row, far right

The Chief's sons help put his body into the simple coffin

Family members and friends file past the body of Senior Chief Koinange, lying in state at his home in Kiambaa

31 July 1960. His funeral was attended by the largest crowd to that date

Peter Mbiyu, meanwhile, threw himself into the Independent Schools' movement, drumming up support and collecting funds by touring all over Gikuyu county. His brief tenure as president of the independent schools system would be cut short by two key events that were to change the course of future Kenyan politics. The first was World War II, which diverted the world's attention to events in Europe and the Far East. The second was the return of his old friend and London colleague, Jomo Kenyatta, for whom Mbiyu would relinquish the prestigious position as head of the Kenya Teachers' College.

8

Signs of a Revolution

World War II meant that thousands of Africans were 'enlisted', albeit against their will, to serve in various divisions overseas, some of them as far away as Burma as well as various other countries in the Far East. There they were subjected to all kinds of horrific conditions, and many of them died and were forgotten even as the Allies advanced against Hitler and his 'superior' army in Berlin. But those who did survive and did eventually return, came back with different attitudes and feelings towards the settlers than ever before. In combat, they'd seen that a white man bled and died just as often and as much as they did, and the conditions were brutal to all alike. This feeling of 'equality' was to play a critical role in the period leading to and during the State of Emergency.

Meanwhile, by the time the war had come to an end, so too was the self-imposed exile of Mbiyu's good friend, Kenyatta. He'd spent the better part of 15 years in Europe, mostly England, married a British woman, fathered two children, and now was about to return home and join in the post-war movement that was fast taking shape in Kenya. He left England on a warm summer's day in 1946, leaving behind a chapter in his life he knew he could never return to because, in colonial Kenya, an African with a European wife and children of mixed parentage would have complicated things much further. The arrival of Kenyatta off a ship at the harbour in Mombasa in December 1946 was of great significance, not only for the KCA (which was now KAU) but for all of Kenya's Africans. Old KCA colleagues and neighbours streamed in for the celebrations organised by Kenyatta's loyal friend and colleague, Peter Mbiyu Koinange.

As Mbiyu later recalled:

'The homecoming for Jomo was psychologically a dramatic climax of several events. It happened immediately after the end of the war. When the Afro-European friendly relations created by the troops in Burma were still alive, the KAU was two years old. Trade Unions were being established and the Kenya African Farmers Associations were springing up like mushrooms. What Africans earned during the war was still in their pockets. At the African District Councils in the Central Province of Kenya and in Tribunal Courts, councillors were debating the country's affairs with mutual respect. All this was happening when Jomo stepped off the ship on that December morning in 1946.

'Jomo Kenyatta was accorded a tumultuous welcome. Even he did not expect such an organised, jubilant reception. Excited people had thronged the railway station hours before the train arrived. They all wanted to have a glance at Jomo. When he arrived, we snatched him through the thick mass of excited people and into a taxi which sped at fifty miles an hour to avoid unnecessary trouble which might bring the movement at the station to a standstill. Dagoretti Road was lined up on both sides by children who were waving salute to Jomo. At Waithaka Secondary School we had to stop and hear children sing a special song composed for him.

'At the reception I handed back to Kenyatta the responsibility of looking after his family. One of Jomo's personal wishes was to re-establish himself among his family and relatives. During World War II, Jomo had supervised vegetable production on a farm at Torrington Common, Sussex. This back-to-the-land venture re-kindled in him the basic love of the soil. "For years I dreamt of the place of my birth," he said. "I was going to see my dreams come true. You see, *Kolofi* (the name he affectionately called me), eldership in Kikuyu is meaningless, unless one has a home, a real home. Men in my age-group received me in their homes. I have got to reciprocate it, not in a house built on another man's land but on my legitimate land. At Dagoretti I always feel myself a foreigner and a beggar. I must get myself established at Ichaweri."'[1]

After the celebrations, Kenyatta would make his way to Chief Koinange's home in Banana Hill, where he knew he had unfinished business to tend to.

He knew, despite the fact that he'd spent so much time abroad and had for the most part been cut off from the his tribal affiliations, that the first thing he had to do was to reconcile his claim to leadership with the traditional forces within the tribe. One powerful focus of these tribal feelings lay in the old chief, whom Jeremy Murray-Brown described:

'The Chief, though government-appointed, had earned himself something of the respect tradition accorded to the chiefs of the past, men like Waiyaki and Wangombe.'[2]

Kenyatta therefore set out to make his peace with Koinange and his family. His relationship with the Koinange family was critical to his future plans if he was to pursue any firm political leadership. In the past he had joined in the general KCA abuse and ridicule of Koinange and other government-appointed chiefs, and now the Senior Chief was being singled out by the colonial Administration for further vilification. In London, Kenyatta had appeared to change his attitude, at least towards Mbiyu; now he sought alliance with the Senior Chief.

Koinange also saw the value of having the educated and ambitious Kenyatta as an ally, and quickly welcomed him into his household. As a further sign of their new alliance, the chief offered him one of his daughters, Grace Mitundu, as Kenyatta's third wife. It didn't matter that Kenyatta had left a wife in England, this was more a formality and a rite of passage. With this agreement 'sealed', Kenyatta had established himself politically and socially among the traditional leadership of

Kikuyuland and given the chief a son-in-law who would prove to be a great asset in the fight for independence. Mitundu would later give birth to a baby girl, Jane Wambui, but would die of complications soon after. Wambui would be raised by Kenyatta's fourth wife, Ngina, who also went on to have three children of her own.

Meanwhile, there was much ground to cover on the political front. During the late 1930s there appeared to have been a growing acceptance of the idea of African representation in Britain and among some members of the Administration. In 1938 the British government amended the Kenya constitution to provide for the nomination of two unofficial African members. But the colonial Administration would 'sit' on the matter for a full five years before making any move. In 1943, the government acceded to a request by the Nairobi African Advisory Council that two of its English-speaking members represent it on the Native Affairs Committee, where previously no Africans had been allowed.

All this stirred up a flurry of political activity and heated debate. There followed a barrage of letters to the local press, *Baraza*, and a series of campaigns by potential candidates as the first African Representative to the Legislative Council.

Late in 1943, Koinange's American-educated son, Mbiyu, toured Central and Nyanza Provinces asking chiefs and local native council members to endorse a petition to the Secretary of State, signed by Chief Koinange, asking the Governor to appoint Mbiyu to the Legislative Council. Two things should be noted here: firstly, Koinange's word still commanded respect in just about every corner of the country, and secondly, Koinange himself still held his vision of a political dynasty developing in his family and, with Mbiyu appointed to the Council, this would be a benefit not just to the nation but the family as well.

In announcing the imminent appointment of an African, the Governor appeared to be trying to lessen its impact by affirming that it did not cancel the government's policy of building up African experience of democracy slowly through the Local Native Councils. He would choose the new African member from a list of names compiled by the Chief Native Commissioner, after consultation with all the Local Native Councils and Provincial Councils. Almost immediately the names started pouring in: Henry Kere and Solomon Adagala from the Luhyia tribe, Paul Mboya and Joel Omino from the Luo, Jimmy Jones, Paul Harrison, Jimmy Jeremiah and Harry Stephens from the coast and, on all lists, Mbiyu Koinange and Eluid Mathu from Central Province.

In the end it was a contest between Mbiyu and Mathu. The former was the son of a highly respected chief, the first Kenya African to get a Masters Degree, the result of a dozen years of study in America and Britain, and the founder of the Kenya Teachers College at Githunguri. The latter was the son of a 'retired medicine-man', Boy Scout, Alliance High School and Fort Hare University (South Africa) graduate, Exeter University College and Oxford student, teacher at Alliance and then, after a disagreement with its headmaster, principal of his own school at Waithaka, founder of the Alliance High School Old Boys Club and the Kenya African Teachers Union (KATU), and member of the Race Relations Committee.

Both men were Kiambu Kikuyus, both had been educated overseas and had travelled widely, both were educators, both were experienced with Europeans and fluent in English, and both wanted to be selected. Mbiyu had a head start because of his tours around the nation earlier that year, but Mathu was equally popular and aggressive. He gave speeches, attended Local Native Council meetings, and wrote letters to the press. It was an interesting contest: Mbiyu using his father's friends, his Kikuyu Independent Schools Association connections; Mathu, his Alliance and KATU contacts. In it all was an undertone of the traditional versus the modern.

In the end it was the modern that won. According to some, Mbiyu not only lacked the polish of Mathu, he was basically an 'outsider'. His Kenya Teachers College was too closely related to the independent schools, which were known to have links with the banned KCA. He had been to America, while Mathu had gone to Oxford, which helped the latter both with the government and influential Africans. In a special edition of the *Kenya Gazette*, on 4 October 1944, the governor announced that

Eluid Mathu would be the first African representative in the Legislative Council, or LEGCO as it was popularly known.

Mbiyu would later complain in a book written in 'exile' in America during the Emergency period, entitled *The People of Kenya Speak for Themselves*:

> 'Nineteen of the twenty-six Local Native Councils and nine of the twelve provincial representatives the Government consulted chose me over Mathu, but none of my informants remembered this, and I found no documentary evidence to substantiate this.'[3]

However, it was primarily Gikuyu-based, and now with Kenyatta back and firmly in control at the Kenya Teachers College, ten of them would meet regularly at Koinange's home in Kiambaa, a group that came to be more commonly known as the 'Kiambaa Parliament' and which took on a more radical and militant look.

One of its leaders was Bildad Kaggia, a short, stout man with thick glasses. Born the son of a poor tenant farmer, Kaggia did well in school and was one of a limited number of Africans who qualified for high school. Unfortunately, Kaggia's father couldn't afford to pay for it and the young Kaggia went to work as a clerk for the government. During World War II, he served with the British Army in the Middle East, where he was influenced by black American soldiers who were a lot more sophisticated than he was. Later, when transferred to Britain, he was shocked to see whites actually partaking in physical labour. This further reinforced Kaggia's feelings that with education and equal opportunity, Africans were no different from whites, and this made him even more determined to do something about the plight of his people.

Another individual whose name to this day conjures up images of brutality, and who was considered one of the most militant and later one of the most vicious in the organisation, was Fred Kubai. A trade union leader who was himself half-Gikuyu and half-Giriama, Kubai had, as early as 1949, along with the Indian activist Makhan Singh, publicly demanded independence for Kenya. On 1 May of that year, six trade unions came together in Nairobi to form the East African Trades Union Congress (EATUC). Kubai became president and Makhan Singh became General Secretary. This was an aggressive militant organisation, committed not only to fighting for improved wages and conditions but also to confronting the settlers and the British Administration.

The following year, EATUC raised the demand for independence under majority rule, the first African organisation to make such a demand. The authorities were quick to respond. Kubai, Singh and a dozen other union leaders and activists were arrested. Those still at large called for a general strike, and for nine days Nairobi came to a complete standstill. Large crowds of strikers clashed with police until they were driven off the streets by a massive show of military strength. The strike quickly spread throughout the country, eventually involving some 100,000 workers. The port of Mombasa was closed for two days. The authorities stood firm, however, and the strike was eventually defeated. Makhan Singh, the man held mainly responsible for the insurrection, was detained and put on trial for his involvement in the strike. His trial would go on to last for the better part of the next 11 years. The other union leaders were released over a period, with Kubai being released after eight months in prison.

Upon his release he helped create what was known in Nairobi as the Forty Group (a name derived from their year of initiation), a band of young men most of whom had served in the war and had returned to a nation where they were tenants in their own lands and where they were constantly treated as second-class citizens. Others included John Mungai, another powerful union activist and friend of Kubai, the Senior Chief's sons, Peter and John Mbiyu, and several other influential men.

It was during one of the many meetings of the Kiambaa Parliament that it was decided that in order to take matters to a new level, they would have to create an organisation that would be foolproof to government informers and one that would demand 100 per cent loyalty. Koinange suggested the age-old Gikuyu custom of *muma* or oathing in the style of the *mbari*-system, itself considered a 'coming of age of sorts' for members of a social group (*riika*). The others agreed, but Kubai insisted on making the oath tougher and stricter than that administered within the tribe. After a series of discussions, it was agreed that the oath would be taken only at night and in two stages. The first was relatively harmless and was more an oath of allegiance and secrecy.

The second part was more hands-on and more painful to the initiate. It was more or less patterned after traditional male initiation ceremonies, involving slaughtering a male goat of one solid colour, collecting its blood and cutting out its intestines.

In the words of Karari Njama in his book with Donald Barnett, *Mau Mau from Within*, he talks about how he was initiated into one such secret society:

'We were led into a single hut in the forest. By the light of the lamp, I could see the furious guards who stood armed with *pangas* and *simis*. Right in front of us stood an arch of banana and maize stalks and sugar cane stems tied by a forest creeping and climbing plant.

'We were harassed to take out our coats, money, watches, shoes and other European metal we had in our possession. Then the oath administrator, who had painted his face with white chalk put a band of raw goat's skin on the right wrist of each one of seven persons who were to be initiated. We were then surrounded by goats' small intestines on our shoulders and feet.

'Another person then sprayed us with some beer from his mouth as a blessing, at the same time throwing a mixture of the finger millet with other cereals on us.

'Then the oath administrator pricked our right middle finger with a needle until it bled. He then brought the chest of a Billy-goat and its heart still attached to the lungs and smeared them with our blood. He then took a Gikuyu gourd containing blood and with it made a cross on our foreheads and on all important joints saying, 'May this blood mark the faithful and brave members of Gikuyu and Mumbi Unity; may this same blood warn you that if you betray our secrets or violate the oath, our members will come and cut you into little pieces at the joints marked by this blood.

'We were then asked to lick each other's blood from our middle fingers and vow after the administrator: 'If I reveal this secret of Gikuyu and Mumbi to a person not a member, may this blood kill me. If I violate any of the rules of the oath may this blood kill me. If I lie, may this blood kill me.'

'We were then ordered to hold each other's right hand and in that position, making a line, passed through the arch seven times. Each time the administrator cut off a piece of the goat's small intestines, breaking it into pieces, while all the rest in the hut repeated a curse on us:

'"*Tathu! Ugotuika ungiaria maheni! Muma uroria muaria ma*" (translation: 'Slash! May you be cut like this! Let this oath kill he who lies.')

'We were then made to stand facing Mount Kenya, encircled by intestines, and given two dampened soil balls and ordered to hold the left-hand soil ball against our navels.

'We then swore, "I swear before God and before all the people here that ... I shall never reveal the secret of the KCA oath, which is of Gikuyu and Mumbi and which demands land and Freedom, to any person who is not a member of our society. If I ever reveal it, may this oath kill me!" (Repeated after each vow while biting the chest-meat of a Billy-goat held together with the heart and lungs.)

'"I shall always help any member of our society who is in difficulty or in need of help.

'"If I am ever called, during the day or night, to do any work for this society, I shall obey.

'"I shall on no account ever disobey the leaders of this society.

'"If I am ever given firearms or ammunition to hide, I shall do so.

'"I shall always give money or goods to this society whenever called upon to do so.

'"I shall never sell land to a European or an Asian.

'"I shall not permit intermarriage between Africans and the Whites.

'"I will never go with a prostitute.

'"I shall never cause a girl to become pregnant and leave her unmarried.

'"I will never marry and seek a divorce.

'"I shall never allow any daughter to remain uncircumcised.

'"I shall never drink European manufactured beer or cigarettes.

'"I shall never help the missionaries in their Christian faith to ruin our traditional and cultural customs.

'"I shall never steal any property belonging to a member of our society.

'"I shall obey any strike call whenever notified.

'"I will never retreat or abandon any of our mentioned demands but will daily increase more and stronger demands until we achieve our goals.

'"Last but not least, I shall always follow the leadership of Jomo Kenyatta and Mbiyu Koinange."

'We repeated the oath while pricking the eye of a goat with a ki-apple thorn seven times and then ended the vows by pricking seven times some Sodom-apples. To end the ceremony, blood mixed with some good-smelling oil was used to make a cross on our foreheads indicating our reception as members of Gikuyu and Mumbi warning us: Forward ever and backward never.'[4]

Several things should be noted here: firstly, the number seven is considered ominous and evil by the Gikuyu. Secondly, this particular oath was only one of several variations that were applied throughout the 1930s, 1940s and 1950s. Thirdly, Karari Njama, among others, confirms what has been the subject of countless whispered conversations concerning who were the key players behind this movement, namely Koinange and Kenyatta amongst others.

Meanwhile, rumours began circulating at about this time of a secret society known as *Andu A Ndemwa Ithatu* (People of the

Three Letters). No one could pinpoint its origin but it was determined that oathing only took place at night and in total secrecy. The name appeared again after the local Special Branch Police broke into a secret oathing ceremony. The oath administrator turned to his initiates shouting, '*Mau Mau! Mau Mau!*'.[5] Asked about the meaning of the words, no one could say since it wasn't a language anyone understood. (Later they were told that the Gikuyu have a system of interchanging words, a game that uncircumcised boys used to play when they would flip letters around and make new words out of them. Later, this would come in handy as a way of intentionally misleading outsiders.)

They were told that '*Mau Mau*' actually meant '*Uma Uma*', meaning 'Leave, Leave' or 'Get Out, Get Out'. Later, when the government put two and two together they concluded that '*Mau Mau*' and '*Uma Uma*' could very well be one and the same. Other informants suggested that '*Mau Mau*' stood for the Swahili words '*Mzungu Arudi Uingereza, Mwafrika Apate Uhuru*', meaning 'Let the European return to Europe and the African obtain his freedom'. (The 'Get Out, Get Out' concept could also have applied here to mean 'Get out of our country'.)

Others still have suggested that this name was a mispronunciation by a Maasai initiate who had been arrested in the town of Naivasha, 100 miles from Nairobi. Asked what he had been engaging in, he replied that he had partaken in *mumau* instead of *muma*, the Gikuyu word for oath taking. The arresting officer had in turn misspelled the name in his report, calling it *Mau Mau*.

Yet another explanation for the name came from none other than a Gikuyu chief from Nyeri, a government informer who told his long-time friend and British army colonel, Richard Meinertzhagen, who had been in the country since the early 1900s and had his own contacts within the tribe:

> 'The chief tells me he fears an outbreak of violence against Europeans involving murders on a large scale under the direction of a secret society now in existence called '*Maw Maw*' whose influence in the tribe is rapidly growing and whose oaths, taken in utmost secrecy, are binding on those who are compelled to take them.'[6]

He immediately wrote to the Governor, informing him of this potentially serious situation. He even delivered the letter personally to the Governor's office, but he neither received a reply nor was it ever followed up ... until much later.

What must be understood, and this is a subject that's been thoroughly dissected in institutions of higher learning worldwide, is that *Mau Mau*, or whatever the movement wished to call itself, came out of a people pushed to the limit of their physical and mental endurance. It was a case of 'desperate actions calling for desperate measures', and the Gikuyu and all others involved in the movement reacted in the only way left open to them.

A half-century before, when the British were laying down tracks for the 'iron snake' that was to link the coast and the source of the Nile, the Gikuyu had for the most part welcomed them and given them all the accommodation they required. But when the British continued exploiting the land and its riches they were doing what they'd done in their other colonies; they were encroaching and laying claims to land that was already legitimately occupied.

They then ungraciously, and many times at gunpoint, dispossessed the original landowners, thereby making them tenants on their own land. As the African population continued to grow, land or lack of it, increasingly became the burning issue. The colonial Administration thought that they could bully their 'subjects' into submission, but they had grossly miscalculated the power and strength of the African spirit, especially when pushed to the limit. *Mau Mau* was a final resort of a people left with no alternative.

The British, on the other hand, saw it as an opportunity to reinforce their military might as well as their paternalistic attitude towards their 'subjects'. But they needed an excuse, a reason to 'justify' their actions; they sought to do this through an extremely successful system known as the propaganda machine. Their first task was to portray *Mau Mau* as a band of bloodthirsty, atavistic, sub-human 'savages' who worshipped the devil and who were going to return to the savagery that pervaded all of Africa before European colonisation. In a word, they had to be put down by necessary force. It didn't matter that this same group being referred to as 'savages' was the same one that had been so co-operative and accommodating of the settlers when they first arrived. Furthermore, no one bothered to make the effort to get to the root cause of the unrest. It was typical colonial mentality at work, namely that there was no way these inferior natives could band together to form any kind of threat against the 'Mighty British' empire. It was, looking back, a costly mistake that would hit the British where it hurt the most and later cause untold devastation in terms of lives and property, eventually leading to the downfall of an empire.

Initially, oathing took place only in Kiambu district, in particular at Senior Chief Koinange's residence, which was by this time a hive of activity. Taxi-loads of people would be hauled in at all hours of the night as the 'Kiambu Parliament' continued to expand its membership. The acquisition of guns and ammunition was a priority and, since the government had long ago passed laws prohibiting Africans from possessing or carrying firearms, it became necessary to build an armoury inside Koinange's house to be used as a weapons cache.

The man put in charge of this was Stanley Mathenge, a medium-built, stocky individual who would later play a prominent role in the movement. Mathenge's men would follow a lone policeman, waiting for a chance to steal his weapon. If the policeman resisted, he would be killed and his body dismembered and buried in remote places.

Because no bodies were ever found, officials were led to believe that the missing, who were mostly recruited from the distant Northern Frontier District, had quite simply gone home. Meanwhile Kubai, Mungai and others insisted on spreading the oath to Nairobi and other populated areas, a view that brought resistance from the other members, who argued that it was still too early for this and that things would get out of hand if they went unsupervised. The Kiambaa Parliament was being very cautious in trying to maintain the most important aspect of this society, namely its anonymity. So insistent was Koinange on the issue of secrecy that when one day in 1950 one of his own sons, David Gathiomi, accidentally shot and killed himself while cleaning a loaded rifle in the chief's house, he had to be buried underneath the house and in total secrecy to avoid any kind of government suspicion. This was one of the family's saddest but best kept secrets, and one they had to live with for a long time. Gathiomi left behind a wife and two young children.

Needless to say, the die had been cast and there was nothing to stop the growth of the movement then. Oathing continued to spread and the secret society began to split into various cells – each independent of the other, but all with the same common principles and goals. Oathing may have varied slightly depending on where and who administered it, but the content was consistent for the most part.

The most notable and uncompromising oath-administrator in the Kiambu region was John Westley Mbiyu. In many ways he was a lot like his father, Koinange; short, of slight build, extremely intelligent and equally ruthless. As the movement took root, John Mbiyu would find himself in charge of sabotaging government installations and creating unrelenting havoc among the settler population in Kiambu.

John Mbiyu waged a personal war against the settler population probably because he felt closest to his father and knew the pain and humiliation the old chief had suffered at the hands of an extremely ungrateful administration. Despite the fact that the chief had selflessly worked for the government and in return received countless awards and medals from the British crown, including the Certificate of Honour and the King's Medal for African chiefs, both outstanding and prestigious awards, the Government, for some inexplicable reason, chose to treat him with the utmost disrespect. As we shall see, John Mbiyu would be at the heart of the crisis that would lead to the Declaration of Emergency.

He also enjoyed the panic that decapitating settler dogs and impaling the heads on stakes before placing them at the gates of settlers' homes would create. This was a form of intimidation that proved very effective and bothersome to the animal-loving settlers. Pretty soon many settlers began to walk around their homes with guns strapped to their waists. Shotguns, loaded and ready, lay on their dining tables.

Meanwhile, the oathing process took on a life of its own. Koinange, Kenyatta, and John Mbiyu did their best to try to contain it, but a group that included Kubai, Job Muchuchu, Stanley Mathenge and James Beauttah felt it was natural for the movement to spread across the inter-tribal board. Incidents of oathing were soon reported in Nairobi and Thika, Murang'a, Nyeri and Embu as late as 1948.

Despite the rumours flying all over the halls of government about a secret society and mass oathing, there appeared a general reluctance on the part of the colonial Administration to acknowledge the situation. They would neither own up and admit to their lack of knowledge, nor prove that there was indeed 'trouble brewing' in the reserves.

The government tried to point fingers at KAU (whose leaders consisted mostly of ex-KCA members) by accusing them of being behind the so-called movement. The question was further put to the two African representatives in Britain, Peter Mbiyu, representing KAU, and Eliud Mathu, representing LEGCO, both at Whitehall, to petition the organisation's grievances against the colonial Administration. They both denied that *Mau Mau* existed and insisted they had no knowledge of any secret oathing.

This statement by Peter Mbiyu and his obvious relationship to the Administration's chief nemesis, his father, would later prohibit him from re-entry into Kenya during the Emergency period and he would end up spending a decade in Europe and the United States, all the while defending *Mau Mau* and petitioning for his family's and his colleagues' release from detention. (He would also go on to write several papers and a book, *The People of Kenya Speak for Themselves*, in which he outlined just what had driven his people into the predicament they were in.)

9

State of Emergency

By early 1949, *Mau Mau* had taken on a dramatic and deadly approach. No one knows who gave the actual order to escalate matters to a new level. Perhaps it was a rogue unit that was tired of 'petty' intimidation, or it may have been an order that 'came directly from the top'. Whatever the reason, the action was swift, ruthless and deadly. Late one July evening, the movement claimed its first settler victim, an old farmer who lived alone and treated his domestic help with the utmost contempt. The old man was just settling for a bath when his door was smashed down. Before he could go for his gun, he was struck down by the machete-wielding intruders, who then proceeded to hack him to pieces. The authorities arrived the next day and one of them accidentally pulled the bathtub plug; most of the settler's blood and guts trickled down the drain!

During the next few months, several similar murders of settler farmers continued almost unabated. Finally, after the settler population threatened to storm the Governor's home in Nairobi, the government finally had to acknowledge that there did in fact exist a society that, in their words, 'was threatening the national security of the state'. It didn't matter that loyal Gikuyu and other tribesmen were losing their lives daily to this growing menace; when the lives of their own were in danger, the response was quick and drastic. Reports were sent out to all divisional chiefs and headmen, particularly in the Gikuyu Reserve and outlying areas, to be wary of any strange activities happening at night and to report any suspicious goings-on.

Leaders of KAU, including Koinange, Kenyatta, Bildad Kaggia, Paul Ngei and Kumbu Chokwe, were now constantly followed and their movements were monitored by the government. The latter also began to apply pressure on these leaders to publicly denounce *Mau Mau* while at the same time instructing the chiefs and headmen to begin 'de-oathing' their subjects. Senior Chiefs such as Waruhiu were put in charge of making sure that anyone even remotely associated with *Mau Mau* was immediately exposed and arrested.

Kenyatta, Eliud Mathu, Koinange and Chief Josiah Njonjo, another powerful 'Kiambu Parliamentarian', were all forced to tour the country and publicly denounce and distance themselves from anything that smacked of *Mau Mau*. Initially, this was to no avail as none of the leaders wanted to be the first to admit publicly that such a movement existed. The breakaway cells of *Mau Mau* had also sent subtle warnings to the chiefs and other elders to desist from putting down the Movement in any way or they would be regarded as traitors. But government pressure continued to put the squeeze on them, resulting in a no-win situation. At one such gathering, Kenyatta displayed the diplomacy that he would be famous for in years to come. While not directly denouncing the movement, he chose instead to ask a gathering at one such ceremony: 'What is this thing called *Mau Mau*? I have never heard of this name. If it exists, why have we not heard about it? It must be something that does not exist, and therefore we refuse to acknowledge something that's not there.'[1] Reports of Kenyatta's skirting of the subject angered the authorities, who stepped up pressure, threatening to arrest and imprison him along with the rest of the leaders, whom they claimed they knew very well.

Senior Chief Waruhiu-Wa-Kungu, meanwhile, went about publicly denouncing the movement, claiming that it was causing a disruption in development and that it stood in the way of colonial-African relations. This view was echoed by another government-appointed chief, Nderi, in Nyeri. They set about conducting de-oathing campaigns and used the recruits, known as Homeguards, to help try to rid the government of the impending threat. As Waruhiu continued trashing the movement openly and unabashedly, he began to receive death threats saying he would be a casualty if he did not refrain from his outspokenness.

On the night of 13 December 1950, a spear tied to a long wattle pole was thrust at Chief Waruhiu through a window as he lay in bed in his house near Kiambu, but missed its mark. The police were called and with the help of search dogs, were able to arrest the man. The seriousness of the charge was somehow overlooked when the man claimed that he was angry over his wife being fined by the chief for illegal possession of *johi* or local brew.

Waruhiu continued his de-oathing campaign with a fervour even as death threats continued to be issued. He was by then even more aware of the danger surrounding him and travelled everywhere with bodyguards and a gun concealed in his jacket.

By early 1952, reports of oathing had intensified all over the Native Reserves, from Embu to Naivasha. The government was constantly under pressure from the outspoken settler population to bring the movement to an immediate halt. The highlands were increasingly an area of great clashes between the settlers and *Mau Mau*, which led to their concern and uneasiness. Settler pressure had a strong and sympathetic ear in London, and the colonial administration didn't want reports reaching Whitehall of their incompetence against an 'obviously inferior gang of savage thugs'.

They therefore focused their pressure on what they termed the ringleaders. They issued an ultimatum to them to either denounce the movement or face the consequences. On 24 August the government called a large meeting in Kiambu, so large that people had been gathering at the site for a full day before the meeting. All the prominent leaders were present, including Koinange, Harry Thuku, Eliud Mathu, Kenyatta, Njonjo, James Gichuru, Fred Kubai and Waruhiu. The colonial Administration was also well represented by the Governor, the District Commissioner, Kiambu, and the Secretary for Native Affairs.

This was no doubt the moment that the stalwart Waruhiu had been awaiting for a long time. He climbed on the platform and, clutching a bunch of tough Kikuyu grass, waved it back and forth saying:

'Kikuyuland is like this grass, blowing one way and another in the breeze of *Mau Mau*. We have come here to denounce this terrible movement; it has spoiled our country and we do not want it. Join me in denouncing this terrible movement.'[2]

Kenyatta came to the microphone. Staring out at the thousands who had turned out to hear their leader speak, he was also aware that this was as big a set-up by the government as had ever happened. He knew his presence and that of the other leaders commanded most, if not all, of Kikuyuland. He knew his words would be heard and interpreted as law.

He began:

'This meeting is of the Gikuyu elders and leaders who have decided to address a public meeting and see what the disease in Kikuyuland is, and how this disease can be cured. We are being harmed by a thing called *Mau Mau*. Who wants to curse *Mau Mau*?'[3]

Every hand in the audience immediately went up. Kenyatta would continue to use this tactic, all the while letting the people do the answering and not wholly committing himself. He also used Gikuyu proverbs skilfully to make his point. He concluded:

'*Mau Mau* has spoiled the country. Let *Mau Mau* perish forever. All people should search for *Mau Mau* and kill it.'[4]

This last comment was a little too scathing of the movement and Kenyatta would later receive a warning by the executive committee to tone down his rhetoric (in other words, no one had the authority to say whatever they wanted). When Kenyatta had finished, Harry Thuku, Eluid Mathu, James Gichuru and Josiah Njonjo wa Mugane all took the microphone and denounced *Mau Mau* with Njonjo saying, 'It will put us back fifty years.'[5]

Then it was the turn of the colonial Administration's most-vehement opponent. Eighty-four-year-old Koinange-wa-Mbiyu faced the Europeans present in front of him with the boldness that had gained him such respect among his people. He singled out one of the colonial officers and began:

'I can remember when the first European came to Kenya. I worked alongside your father, and you are just like my son. In the First World War you asked our young men to go to fight with the British against the Germans, and many were killed. In the Second World War you came again and asked us to fight against the Germans and Italians, and our young people were again ready to serve. Now there are Germans and Italians in Kenya, and they can live and own land in the highlands from which we are banned, because they are white and we are black. What are we to think? I have known this country for eighty-four years. I have worked on it. I have never been able to find a single piece of white land.'[6]

Koinange sat down to a thunderous standing ovation from the crowd and a stunned silence from the Europeans on the podium. He had managed to stick a thorn in the side of the government by going to the core of his people's grievances. Most important, he wasn't about to sell out his people ... he'd never done it as Chief, and he wasn't about to do it now. What he said was true, but it wasn't what the Administration wanted to hear. The authorities didn't forget this and would use this speech against him in the coming months.

In the meantime, it seemed as if certain elements of the movement, particularly a group known as the Forty Group, stemming from the year that the members were circumcised, were not very pleased with the way both Chief Waruhiu and Kenyatta had conducted themselves at the mass meeting. So incensed were they that at a secret emergency meeting they warned Kenyatta that his denunciation had been too strongly worded. And to deter others they embarked on a secret, selected assassination.

Waruhiu had known from the time of the fateful meeting that he was a marked man. To make matters worse, in Kiambu he rivalled the Koinange family in prestige. He was strongly opposed to oathing and, as a Christian, resented the animalistic tendencies that rituals took. On 7 October he made a prophetic public speech at a land trial he'd been summoned to:

> 'There are men who are going to be murdered, they eat with their friends, they laugh with them and they sleep at night. They will die in a short moment and they have known no fear before. Their relatives will weep one day, but then they will be happy again because his life was good. But there are others, they are the murderers, they cannot sit and laugh with their friends and drink tea with them. They think about what they are going to do, and at night they do not sleep, they have no rest. They do their evil things and in the end they will be caught and killed themselves. And their relatives will never forget it and their children will still know about it that their father was an evil man.'[7]

On his way home, sitting in the back of his Hudson, Waruhiu complained to his companions about the reluctance of the recently-arrived Governor, Sir Evelyn Baring, to bring strong action against *Mau Mau*. As his car turned a corner on the hilly road, it was waved to a stop by three men wearing police uniforms. One of the men approached the car and asked if Senior Chief Waruhiu was in the car. Apparently the man was from a different part of Kikuyuland and was not familiar with the chief. As soon as Waruhiu identified himself, the uniformed man drew his weapon and shot him in the face, then several more times in the body. None of the other passengers were harmed. Before leaving the scene, they also blew out one of the tyres of the chief's car, then sped off. The police found him as he had been sitting, in the rear seat with his feet still up on the back of the seat in front.

Shock waves echoed throughout the administration with the execution-style murder of one of their staunchest supporters in broad daylight. The colonial government came out to strongly condemn the 'barbarous' act and at the same time pay tribute to a 'dedicated and loyal servant who had served his government and his people for over 30 years': 'Chief Waruhiu was an inspired leader of men: all have suffered a great loss through his death – his own people, Africans throughout the Colony, and in all Communities.'[8]

But not all communities were mourning this loss. In fact, many Gikuyu were instead celebrating the murder. Some of them even made up songs to mark the occasion, one of which went:

'I will never sell out the country or love money more than my country. Waruhiu sold out his country for money, but he died and left the money.'[9]

In the course of the next few days, and following information received by the CID, two Gikuyu made a series of confessions to two independent magistrates. In these confessions they gave a full account of the assassination of Chief Waruhiu, and the gunman stated he had been given the pistol with instructions to murder Chief Waruhiu by John Westley Mbiyu Koinange, the son of the ex-Chief, at the Chief's home.

The driver of the car also confessed he knew of the plot to kill the chief. On 30 March 1953, John Mbiyu, his stepbrother Noah Karuga and two others, Wahinga and Gathuku, were charged with the murder, and Chief Koinange was implicated as the mastermind behind it. They were all arrested and remanded in custody without bail, pending further investigation. The 84-year-old chief was again to face humiliation in police custody, despite decades of loyalty and dedication to the colonial government.

The Koinange family hired the services of a prominent Indian defence lawyer, Deepak Vohra, who argued that it was totally unnecessary and inappropriate to incarcerate the Chief as there was nowhere he'd be going, and more so because of his extensive dedication to government service and exemplary record, citing the various honours bestowed on him by His Majesty's Government, including the Medal of Honour and the King's Cross. But his appeal fell on deaf ears. The family was to later, with the help of British Members of Parliament Leslie Hale and Fenner Brockway, hire the help of the well-known British solicitor, Dingle Foot.

But it didn't help much that at the same time that the case was in progress, a prominent Nyanza chief sent a most interesting report to the Provincial Commissioner on what he'd been told by Chief Waruhiu, with whom he'd been very close. He professed how the late chief had told him among other things, that 'ex-Senior Chief Koinange and Jomo Kenyatta were the actual ringleaders behind *Mau Mau*, despite and regardless of what anyone said.'[10]

During the course of the trial the gunman and driver recanted their confessions and adduced the defence that their confession had been obtained under duress. The magistrate in his judgement found that both the accused and their witnesses, 'in an effort to get away from their confessions, have told a pack of lies.' On 15 April 1953, they were both found guilty and sentenced to death by hanging. John Mbiyu, his half-brother Noah Karuga and Chief Koinange were all acquitted on the grounds that the evidence of the confession, although admissible, had not received sufficient corroboration to justify a conviction. They were released immediately and the charges against them were dropped; but their freedom would only prove to be temporary.

The murder of Chief Waruhiu set the seal on Governor Sir Evelyn Baring's conclusion that the most drastic action was required. Shortly after his arrival in Nairobi in early October 1952, he went on an extended tour of the affected areas and, on his return, sent a secret cable to the Secretary of State, giving his reasons for the absolute necessity of declaring a State of Emergency under the Emergency Powers Order in Council. Part of his cable read:

'I have just returned from a tour and the position is very serious. The *Mau Mau* movement is like a hydra; it has many heads. There is clear determination by their leaders to destroy all sources of authority. There is evidence that most criminal action is planned in, and instructions are sent from, Kiambu.

'It is now abundantly clear that we are facing a planned revolutionary movement. If the movement cannot be stopped, there will be an administrative breakdown, followed by bloodshed amounting to civil war.

'Absolute unanimity of opinion that the instigators of *Mau Mau* are the leaders of KAU, although some of the leaders of the latter may not be implicated. We are faced with a formidable organisation of violence and, if we wait, the trouble will become much worse and probably lead to the loss of so many lives that in the future bitter memories of bloodshed will bedevil all race relations.'[11]

On 14 October the Secretary of State approved the proposal to declare a State of Emergency, code-named 'Operation Jock Scot', to be followed by the arrest of Jomo Kenyatta and Koinange-wa-Mbiyu and the other leaders of *Mau Mau*. He also approved the reinforcement by air of a British battalion from the Middle East, and the dispatch of a British cruiser to Mombasa. The British battalion would arrive by air on the day the operation would go into effect.

At midnight on 20 October, the inevitable happened. Among the first to be arrested were Koinange-wa-Mbiyu and his son, John Westley Mbiyu, on a charge of having given false evidence in connection with the assassination of Senior Chief Waruhiu. Next on the list was Jomo Kenyatta, who was waiting as the two dozen or so police arrived to take him away.

By the time daybreak came, 187 KAU members, also thought to be members of *Mau Mau*, had been rounded up and arrested, including Eluid Mathu, Kungu Karumba, Paul Ngei, Bildad Kaggia, Fred Kubai, Achieng Oneko, Josiah Njonjo and James Gichuru.

The Koinange family was not in the least bit spared; one of his wives, Joyce Kagendo, was arrested, as were four of her children, Frederick Mbiyu, Edith Muthoni, Noah Karuga and Lilian Wairimu, and other sons and daughters from different wives, James Njoroge, John Westely Mbiyu, Tabitha Muthoni and Josephine Muthoni. In all, the authorities arrested a dozen members of the Koinange family, representing the largest number of persons arrested from a single family unit. Incidentally, Lillian Wairimu died mysteriously while in detention in 1955.

10

The Detention Years

Under the Emergency Powers Act, Senior Chief Koinange was sentenced to nine years in detention in the remote desert town of Marsabit. John Mbiyu was also sentenced to detention in the same place, where he was able to nurse and take care of his ageing father since he didn't have any of his wives around. After a while, the Administration decided that Koinange was receiving preferential treatment and put a stop to it by removing John Mbiyu and sending him to the remote island of Lamu. Frederick Mbiyu was sentenced to seven years in Manyani, another desolate town in the Northern Frontier District. The other family members were sentenced to terms varying from five to nine years in different parts of the country.

The detention years took their toll on the 84-year-old Koinange. He often fell ill from malnutrition and lack of care. His captors didn't take his age into account and would often herd him along with the other younger prisoners and demand of him the same work output as everyone else. They often taunted him and ridiculed him by dressing him in his chief's regalia and parading him in front of the other prisoners, saying, 'Here's your chief. Come and worship your leader who has come to save you.'[1] The humiliated Koinange would retreat to his cell too sick to resist, too bitter to forget all the years of selfless rule and dedication to an administration that was equally myopic and ignorant.

In the meantime, the movement took a bloody turn. Despite the presence of 50,000 well-armed and well-trained British troops fighting a 'rag-tag bunch of ill-trained and ill-equipped savages', it soon became apparent that the hunter oftentimes appeared to be the hunted.

Mau Mau would stake out their victims for days at a time, wait for the opportune moment when the guards had gone on their break or when folks were settling down to their dinner, and strike with a viciousness that showed they were a force to be reckoned with. This couldn't have been done without the help of informants.

What better place to have these than in the domestic help, of whom the settlers had grown so accustomed to having around their homes? After a while, as the situation deteriorated, the settlers would no longer allow their domestic help into their homes or compounds after dark, nor were they allowed into Nairobi or the major towns.

Sir Evelyn Baring had hoped that *Mau Mau* would be suppressed without too much effort, and that in a few months the emergency could in fact be relaxed. He had no concept of how widespread and deep-rooted the movement was, and especially of how determined the Gikuyu were to throw off European rule. Indeed, so inaccurate was his information that he actually seemed to believe that Kenyatta was the sole leader of *Mau Mau*. This was, of course, not true: in fact, it is a well-known fact now that *Mau Mau* gunmen were actually in the process of preparing to assassinate Kenyatta as a collaborator at the time of his arrest.

The British completely underestimated the strength and extent of the rebel organisation and found that the means of repression that they had at hand were completely inadequate. Only the fact that the rebel fighting forces, the Land and Freedom Armies, lacked any modern weapons, is perhaps the only reason that they weren't able to inflict very serious damage on the colonial forces. Their failure to master the rebellion enabled the *Mau Mau* to begin recruiting among other tribes, particularly the Kamba. In Nairobi a secret Kamba committee was established and thousands of Kamba were enrolled in the movement. To some settler leaders this seemed the beginning of the end, and they feared that the rebellion would soon engulf the whole colony.

By that time the rebellion was being taken more seriously in London and was seen as threatening the British position, not just in Kenya but throughout Africa. Troop re-enforcements were drafted, and a new military commander, General Erskine, was appointed.

As well as sustaining the military struggle, it was in Nairobi that the movement conducted its political offensive against the British. The *Mau Mau* leadership in Nairobi organised boycotts of European-owned shops and of European goods, of public transport, and early in 1954 was preparing to call a general strike in the city.

It was in Nairobi that efforts were made to spread the rebellion to other tribal groups. The black trade unions played a vital part in all these activities and were recognised by the British as providing the organisational backbone of the movement in Nairobi. When they moved to crush the movement in the city, it was the trade unions that bore the brunt of the repression.

Perhaps no other single episode had a greater effect on the conduct and course of the emergency than the one known as the Lari Massacre. Lari was a farming area three miles wide and seven miles long located a few miles north of Nairobi, near the edge of the high Kikuyu escarpment, looking down into the Rift Valley. The Kikuyu population of Lari was evenly divided between landowners who were followers of a government loyalist, Chief Luka, and landless people who lived as tenants on the owners' land.

The hostility between these two groups was deep and longstanding. In the early 1940s, more than a thousand Kikuyus had been forced off their land in Tigoni near Kiambu to make way for the encroaching European settlement. Many refused to leave their farms, and as a result the government moved in and levelled the buildings and detained those who resisted. Chief Luka and several dozen of his followers agreed to move and were removed to a place called Lari. With this move, Luka allied himself with the Administration and was now regarded as a loyalist. His supporters were known as the Homeguard; when the emergency period began, these Homeguard would grow in numbers, but at the same time they died in great numbers at the hands of *Mau Mau*, who considered them a worse enemy than the Colonial Forces.

Supporters of *Mau Mau* in Lari planned a series of attacks against Luka, but the government heard wind of this and sent reinforcements to 'protect' their ally. But when the attack didn't occur, the troops were re-assigned to various locations to take care of squatter instability. That same night, about 2,000 squatters attacked the homesteads and turned Lari into a bloodbath. Many loyalists, including Chief Luka and his eight wives, were burned to death in their huts. Others were slashed to death, while still others were shot down as they tried to escape. Men, women and children were hacked to death as the *Mau Mau* continued their onslaught. By the time the loyalist Homeguard recovered from this shock and the army and police reinforcements arrived, the fighting had spread and devastation was everywhere.

Rather than accept the massacre for what it was, that is a carefully planned and well-executed attack, the colonial administration chose to use their skillful propaganda machine to gain public sympathy and in turn let the rest of the world know the extent of the 'savagery' they were faced with. The next day, the government invited the press to witness the carnage, and distributed grisly photographs of horribly burned and mutilated men, women and children, as well as animals. Press reports of the massacre at Lari quickly came to symbolise *Mau Mau* savagery. The effect was obvious, and *Mau Mau* sympathy quickly dwindled.

British tabloids wrote stories about 'innocent, helpless, heroic' whites being 'slaughtered and butchered by fanatical, bestial, satanic and barbaric terrorists who were also degraded and merciless gangsters.'[2] What they failed to publicise is what atrocities the British troops in Kenya were committing without conscience or remorse. It was plain to see that the colonial government had the upper hand and, by appearing as the victim, had managed to seek justification and world-wide support for what they were about to do.

The turning point for the British in the war against *Mau Mau* was Operation Anvil, the clearing of Nairobi. *Mau Mau* activists in the capital were stepping up their thefts of guns and ammunition, while at the same time becoming increasingly violent in destroying loyalist opposition in the city. During one such raid, they came upon a four-year-old boy riding a bicycle outside his home. They pounced on him, decapitating him with a machete without so much as a second thought. It turned out he was the son of à prominent Royal Air Force Officer. The situation in Nairobi became so tense, Governor Baring decided on a citywide sweep. Some 25,000 troops and police occupied the city and screened the entire African population.

While the troops maintained their cordon around Nairobi, police swept through one sector of the city after another. Every conceivable hiding place was checked and broken into if necessary. All Gikuyu, along with related Embu and Meru tribesmen, were interrogated on the spot. Over 15,000 men and women were interned without trial and thousands more, overwhelmingly Gikuyu, were expelled from the city. Anyone carrying a union card was immediately interned. The entire leadership of the Transport and Allied Workers Union and the Domestic and Hotel Workers Union, both *Mau Mau* strongholds, were interned, and the bulk of their membership was expelled from the city to the African reserves or banished to detention camps along the coast.

After the success of Operation Anvil, the British proceeded to restore their control over the settler districts and in the reserves, driving the Land and Freedom Armies into the forests. Over 100,000 Gikuyu squatters were deported from the White Highlands back into the reserves, while in the reserves themselves a programme of compulsory villagisation began. By October 1955, over a million Gikuyu had been forcibly resettled behind barbed-wire fences in these heavily protected villages. *Mau Mau* suspects were arrested in droves, and the number interned eventually reached close to 80,000.

The most savage methods were used in restoring 'Law and Order' in the reserves. Torture was widespread and almost routine. Prisoners were beaten, sometimes mutilated and often murdered out of hand. Operating alongside this unofficial reign of terror was an official policy of mass hangings that rivals any other in British pre-colonial history. In the course of eight years, over 1000 rebels were hanged for offences less than murder. Another 300 were hanged for possessing arms and ammunition, and close to 100 more hanged for administering oaths.

Needless to say, the British government was very concerned about the cost the *Mau Mau* war was accruing both monetarily and in personnel. It's estimated the war was costing the colonial government upwards of £1,000,000 a year, and the East African Protectorate was fast becoming a liability to Whitehall. In fact, World War II hero and then Prime Minister, Winston Churchill, expressed concern at the cost the war was accruing on both the Crown and its protectorate, saying that perhaps negotiation was a possibility:

> 'The tenacity of the hold of *Mau Mau* and the Kikuyu shows that they are not the primitive cowardly people which many imagined them to be, but people of considerable fibre, ability and steel, who could be brought to our side by just and wise treatment.'[3]

But the Colonial Office was not about to negotiate with 'savages', and in 1955 launched a counter-attack to Operation Anvil, code-named 'Hammer'. Despite their superiority in weapons, the British troops were very poorly prepared for forest fighting, and at times it appeared that the rebels were getting the better of the vast superior colonial forces. Not gaining the results they wanted from the efforts they were putting in, the British countered with one operation after another, with the intention of crushing the rebels. In the end *Mau Mau*, cut off from supplies and ammunition, one by one began to consider surrender and, in early 1956, they let it be known to the British that they might support a ceasefire so that a discussion of surrender with amnesty could take place.

Ironically, *Mau Mau* leaders met with British officials at the Koinange home in Kiambaa for several weeks of top-secret negotiations conducted by Charles Karuga Koinange, another of the Chief's sons, who had been appointed chief of southern

Kiambu after his father's imprisonment and who had won the confidence of the Europeans.

One of the terms of a possible surrender was the immediate release of the chief and other prominent leaders. As a result of the meetings, almost 100,000 *Mau Mau* actually surrendered, but it seemed more apparent, as the days went by, that the British weren't holding up to their end of the bargain.

In particular, the release of Koinange, Kenyatta, Kubai, Njonjo, Gichuru, Kaggia and others would be difficult to explain to the growing settler resentment. After countless hours of wrangling between the government and the *Mau Mau* leaders with no results, talks were called off and both sides parted with mutual enmity.

Charles Koinange then sought the help of his long-time family friend, Fenner Brockway, the famous British Socialist Member of Parliament. Brockway immediately flew to Nairobi with his solicitor friend, Leslie Hale, and immediately began to organise a series of meetings with the Governor and the Colonial Secretary to help secure Koinange's release. As he was to later record in his book *Outside the Right*, Brockway recounted:

> 'The most moving of our experiences was a visit to old ex-chief Koinange in prison. We sat in the office of a prison official, a young Englishman in tunic and shorts, who continued with his papers as we talked. The ex-chief clung to me and embraced me. We sat in chairs in a group, the old man was very little concerned about himself. "I have had my allotted span," he said simply. "My mind is on my future life." But he was broken by the tragedy which had come to Kenya and anxious for his family. It was pathetic to hear of the pleasure which the news of our visit to his home had given him.'[4]

Meanwhile, the damage to the rebel stronghold had already been done. In the face of such massive opposition and repression the rebellion was broken, and the battered remnants of the Land and Freedom Armies were driven back deeper into the Aberdare Forest. In the course of the fighting the police and military suffered some 600 casualties, of whom only 63 were white. Rebel losses were officially put at 11,003, but it's common knowledge that they were much higher, some estimates going as high as 50,000. Moreover, it ended up costing the British government over £55,000,000 to eventually put down the revolution. Although the rebellion is often portrayed as an almost cannibalistic orgy of rape and murder against defenceless white settlers, the reality is that only 32 of the settlers were killed, a small number in comparison with the casualties on the other side. This disparity indicates both the overwhelming superiority of British firepower and the courage and determination of the rebels in the face of this superiority.

The prisoners in Marsabit had slowly been banding together and rallying for better treatment by the colonial guard. They demanded better sanitary conditions and more hygienic sleeping quarters. They chose as their spokesman Koinange, who despite his age and ill health still had a very keen and sound mind. The octogenarian did what he'd done most of his life, which was to stand up for his people and fight for equality and fair treatment. But again the authorities snubbed him, and even at this late stage decided that before they had an insurrection on their hands, they'd best nip it in the bud.

At midnight on 4 August 1959, Koinange was whisked away from the detention camp, put on a military plane and transferred to Kabarnet in the Turkana region of the country, where temperatures on any given day could reach a scorching 40°C. There, perhaps due to total isolation and loneliness or as some people say, 'The secrets of *Mau Mau* must die with its founders', or perhaps the government had slowly been neglecting him with deliberate intention, Koinange's condition drastically deteriorated.

His son, John Westley Mbiyu, had to be flown in to try to give him moral support, and John's wife, Pauline Njogu, was also flown in by military plane from the women's detention camp in Marsabit to tend to her father-in-law since she had nursing experience.

The last thing the colonial government wanted was to have someone of Koinange's stature die on their hands; it would give the Gikuyu every reason to take up arms again, and this time the cost would probably be more than the British government could afford to handle. In the meantime, another of Koinange's daughters, Margaret Wangui, was in nursing school in England and had just attended a function honouring visiting members of the United Nations. Purely by chance, it was there that she bumped into a familiar family friend, the now Under-Secretary of the United Nations, Ralph Bunche Jr. Margaret had been told as a young girl about Bunche and how he'd spent time at her father's home in Kiambaa many years earlier.

She remembered the way her aunts and uncles had marvelled at his 'western mannerism', how they laughed at his attempts at speaking Gikuyu and how her father had treated him as one of his sons. She also remembered that they'd referred to him as Kariuki, meaning 'he who has returned from the dead'.

She pulled Bunche aside and told him about the situation at Kabarnet and the suffering her father was going through. She ended by asking him to seek an audience with the Colonial Secretary and suggest that Koinange be released and, in her words, 'be brought home to die.'[5]

Bunche was shocked and dismayed at learning how sad things had turned out in the country he'd grown to love all those years ago. He was angered by the callousness and brutality of how such a cowardly administration had imprisoned a man who was nearly 90 years old and who had obviously more than paid for by whatever wrongdoing he'd been accused of. The very next morning he teamed up with Fenner Brockway, and together they wrote to the Colonial Secretary and pleaded for the release of the old chief. Brockway recanted his frustrations in his memoirs:

'I received a message that the old chief was suffering, because of his age. I tried to get Mr Lennox-Boyd (Colonial Secretary) to allow the old chief out under conditions of "house arrest" so that he could be at home. Both the governor and the colonial secretary refused. The utmost concession I could get was permission for one of his wives to join him. Later news came that he was seriously ill. I got permission for his son, Mbiyu, who was in London, to visit him and raised the money for him to go. The old man got worse. I begged the government to allow him to return to his farm for his last days. I had another refusal. Then news came that he had been taken by 'plane and ambulance to the farm. I knew it was to die. It was one of the most unforgivable things I have ever known. I find it very difficult to think kindly of the governor and the colonial secretary who ordered the ex-chief's detention.'[6]

It was meant to be a secret mission, but word got around that Koinange was going to be brought home. The route from Nairobi Airport to his home in Kiambaa, a distance of 64 kilometres, was lined from end to end with supporters. Many of them carried banana trees which signified the respect still held for this great leader. Women ululated endlessly and men waved machetes defiantly as everyone strained to catch a glimpse of the man the colonial government had dubbed 'the Evil Genius of Kikuyuland',[7] a comment echoed by the Chief Native Officer, H. E. Lambert, in describing Koinange:

'A microcosm of quintessential Kikuyudom. To my mind he's loyal to government and only treads consciously on its corns for his own advantage, which may come to the same thing. He is certainly the "Nigger in the Wattle" in government affairs. He has a finger in every pie and there can be little doubt that he has, in the past, managed to pull out many a plum. He has many likeable qualities. He's a great protagonist of Kikuyu Colonialism and (though he doesn't openly admit it) Kikuyu Imperialism. I believe the best way to deal with Koinange is to put all your cards on the table and turn your sleeves up (not in aggression but as evidence that you have nothing to hide) and then to invite him to follow suit. Mutual distrust is the great stumbling block to good administration in Kiambu.'[8]

11

Coming Home to Die

The sickly Koinange came home to a family suffering the effects of long detentions. One thing the colonial government had succeeded in doing was making sure the Koinange family was rendered ineffective during the emergency period. The effects of this were everywhere. Nowhere was there a sign of leadership or opposition to the government. The only son in any position of authority was Charles Karuga, now Chief of Kiambu District. Others like John Westley Mbiyu, Noah Karuga, Frederick Mbiyu and Joyce Kagendo, were still serving out their sentences at the various concentration camps across the country. (One of them, Lillian Wairimu, died mysteriously while in detention.)

As for Peter Mbiyu, he'd been in London when the Emergency period broke out. He made an attempt to head home immediately, but then realised that his services would probably be more valuable where he was than in a detention camp. He spent the better part of the next ten years in Europe and the United States, all the while fighting for the release of his family and comrades. While in the States he took time out to write a manuscript which he intended sending to anyone and everyone who would listen to his condemnation of the colonial government. Peter Mbiyu's book *The People of Kenya Speak for Themselves*, was a tribute to his people with whom he'd felt so isolated and alienated from and yet at the same time so close to. He realised he'd spent the majority of his adult life abroad and had lost so much contact with his roots. Perhaps this was a way of coming to terms with his past. He also teamed up with other 'Foreign Kenyans', among them Tom Mboya and Julius Kiano, and helped write another book. This one called for the release of all their jailed leaders, and was appropriately titled *Struggle for Release of Jomo and his Colleagues*. The book was a bestseller abroad. In it, Mbiyu wrote:

'I visited Paris in 1948 and again 1951, attending or rather lobbying the UNO delegates in the General Assembly at the Palais de Chaillot. Since November 1951, I have been in England as an official representative of the Kenya African Union in the United Kingdom until June 8th when our political organisation was proscribed by the Kenya government. The situation in East and Central Africa is very serious. It amounts to a civil war with the *Agikuyu* people. More than two thousand people have lost their lives, been killed, assassinated, murdered, hanged or starved to death. Causes are both economic and political frustration ... both the government and African are to blame. It will be misleading to regard either the African or the government as angels without a blame. They are all involved... Some of us believe that a solution can be found if Africans are permitted to approach their own people to stop violence. Security of African land tenure, raising standards of living, compulsory education for children of all races will go a long way to ameliorate the present situation. Screening, undiscriminating and collective punishment and shooting is only intensifying bitterness. It is a problem of human relationship and conflict of values and interests. That the present crisis can be solved without further bloodshed is possible, I think. To do so, one should not identify himself either with those using violence or the loyalists, but must establish (with clean hands) a separate camp for those Africans and Europeans sincerely interested in saving lives but not killing.'[1]

This so angered the colonial government 10,000 miles away, that Mbiyu was not allowed to return home until his father's condition worsened considerably.

Meanwhile, Koinange's health was fast taking a turn for the worse. In May 1960, he summoned his household to a gathering and, in between bouts of strained breathing brought about by an advanced stage of pneumonia, he announced in a whispered tone that he did not have very long to live.

According to Pauline Njogu, John Westley Mbiyu's wife:

'He was very sick. He was never the same after they brought him back from that horrible place. They'd reduced him to the status of an animal ... he was a shell of his old self ... it was so sad to see him like this.'[2]

For the next six weeks, it was as though the word had spread throughout Kikuyuland that Koinange was on his deathbed. Every day busloads of people from as far away as Mombasa in the east to Kisumu in the west and everywhere in between would file into the Chief's residence hoping to see him, touch him or at least get his blessings. It had taken a lifetime, but people in the end realised that his loyalty lay unquestionably with his people.

John Westley Mbiyu, who'd been released and was constantly at his side, remembered:

'He was a visionary. He could see farther into the future than anyone could ever imagine or believe; that's why people always questioned his judgement and second guessed his decisions. He accepted the coming of the white man because he knew that it was inevitable; knew that the sooner we befriended this ghost-child the better it would be for the Gikuyu.

'My father's father, Gathecha, had sworn blood-brotherhood with the first foreigner in this land. Now this same foreigner had taken over our land. What were we supposed to do?

'My father was driven off his ancestral home by these greedy, selfish, ruthless bastards who deceived us with their tales of Christianity and how they'd come to save us from eternal death.

'These are the same people who refused to accept my father into the Church, saying he had to give up all but one of his wives. In the beginning, I was very angry with my father for giving in so readily to the white man. What I didn't realize is that my father had known all along that the time had come for the Gikuyu to stop fighting and start surviving.'[3]

This friendly nature had, once again, been perceived as a sign of weakness on the part of the 'mighty Kikuyu', and it was only a matter of time before the Bible-bearing, God-fearing, fire-and-brimstone, men of the cloth had conquered yet another people for 'Queen and country'.

Joseph Karuga Koinange, son of Koinange's second wife, Julia, recalls vividly the events of 27 July 1960.

'I remember that day like it was yesterday. I had been in London studying for my examinations and knew that my father had been ill for a while. I'd made it a point to leave school at the end of the week to catch the weekly flight to Nairobi. I finished my exams and headed to the airport and caught my flight without any problems. On arrival at Embakasi, I was greeted by Frederick Mbiyu who had organised with friends he knew to pass me quickly through customs and out into an awaiting taxi for the two-hour drive home. On the way, Mbiyu informed me of the seriousness of my father's condition and confirmed that he didn't have long to live.

'I contemplated what all this meant and couldn't fathom the idea of life ever being the same without the Old Man. We finally arrived at Kiambaa and there in the yard were hoards of people gathered in small groups talking. They waved me through and I went directly to the master bedroom. There, on the bed, sitting up but looking frail and weak was the grand old man I'd always seen as invincible. He looked a shadow of his former self but his eyes were still alive and fierce as ever. He suddenly stopped what he was doing and stared right at me and whispered, "You made it, my son. I have been waiting for you. Now I can depart." And that was it. He was gone but his eyes kept staring at me. I'll never forget that look.'[4]

A great man had passed away that cold July evening in 1960. Apart from Karuga, his other sons, John Westley Mbiyu, Peter Mbiyu, Frederick Mbiyu, Charles Karuga, and James Njoroge were at his side. Among his wives, Mariamu Wambui, Joyce Kagendo, Elizabeth Gathoni and Julia Njeri were present.

Jomo Kenyatta, newly released from detention, was among the first to arrive upon receiving the news. By the end of the day, word had spread of the passing of a great patriot. Crowds of people began arriving by nightfall and there was a strong police presence in the area to prevent any type of violence from occurring.

For the next seven days, as the body lay in state under government instructions, thousands and thousands of people flocked to Kiambaa, some from as far away as England and the United States, to see for themselves and also pay tribute to this great son of Kenya; a man described in the local *Daily* as 'an icon and a patriarch, a visionary and a luminary, a legend among his people, and most of all a champion of freedom and equality.'[5]

Koinange's funeral was one of the largest ever attended in pre-colonial Kenya. Even though the Emergency period was not officially over, thousands defied the order and came to bid farewell to one of their own. His casket was carried into the church at Kiambaa by six of his sons, three on either side, while his wives and other children occupied the entire first six rows of seats. A potential fiasco was avoided earlier the same morning, when the pastor of the church had questioned Koinange's polygamous lifestyle, but when told of the former chief's devotion and dedication to Christianity, had quickly retracted his objections.

Others present at the funeral included the Governor of Kenya Colony, Sir Evelyn Baring, the Under-Secretary of the United Nations and close family friend, Ralph Bunche Jr, who was recognised by some of those present as the 'young Kariuki' who'd stayed in the chief's home all those years ago and constantly reminded the people of someone who had come back from the dead (thus the name).

British Members of Parliament and close Koinange friends, Fenner Brockway and Leslie Hale, Canon Harry Leakey, S. H. Fazan, Koinange's friend and interpreter in England, Ghanaian President Kwame Nkrumah, a close friend of Peter Mbiyu, Jomo Kenyatta, Tom Mboya, Odinga Oginga, many hundreds of other dignitaries and thousands of friends. As one of his many nephews, Arthur Koinange recalls:

> 'It had been a bright, sunny day and the sun was high in the sky all morning and throughout the funeral service. Suddenly, just as the casket was about to be lowered into the grave, dark grey clouds covered the afternoon sky and a light drizzle began to fall steadily. With the sun still shining, it was a strange sight to behold and many present felt and, believed that this was the passing of a truly blessed son of Kenya.'[6]

He did not live to see the day but, just as in the eyes of the world, yesterday's villains are more often than not the heroes of today – and vice versa – with Kenya's independence in 1963 many of the street names in Nairobi which had previously honoured past colonial commissioners, governors and white pioneers of note, were renamed to honour those who had fought for the country's freedom from colonialism and, in the long term, won.

Hardinge Street, for Sir Arthur H. Hardinge (1897), was then renamed Kimathi Street for the Kikuyu freedom fighter Dedan Kimathi. Stewart Street, for Sir Donald Stewart (1904) became Muindi Mbingu Street, and Senior Chief Koinange-wa-Mbiyu's name would be perpetuated in the former Sadler Street which, before then, had honoured Sir James Hayes-Sadler (1905). It is a busy and usually traffic- and pedestrian-thronged thoroughfare, transformed towards each year-end by the spectacular flowering of its few remaining jacaranda trees.

Harry Thuku's name was to be commemorated in the road where the infamous 'Harry Thuku Incident' took place in 1922 in front of the Norfolk Hotel. Ralph Bunche Jr's name replaced that of Sir E. P. C. Girouard (1909–12), in Girouard Road.

Other significant name changes would include Kenyatta Avenue, replacing the former Delamere Avenue which, before then, had honoured the white pioneer farmer and politician Lord Hugh Delamere – the third baron.

Almost three and a half years to the day after Koinange died, the colonial British East Africa became *Jamhuri ya Kenya*, the Republic of Kenya, on 12 December 1963. Leading the celebrations was none other than Koinange's son-in-law, Jomo Kenyatta, the newly elected Prime Minister. Six months later Kenya was granted *Madaraka* or internal self-government, and once again citizens across the board celebrated their hard-fought struggle for independence. Kenyatta promised freedom for all and stressed forgiveness rather than hate. A quintessential politician, he never lost sight of those who had helped him along the way, and rewarded many freedom fighters handsomely with land and other spoils.

Kenyatta at the same time kept a tight inner circle of close associates, among them his brother-in-law and best friend, Peter Mbiyu Koinange, whom he appointed Minister of State in the Office of the President (where he remained until Kenyatta's death in 1978, thereafter as Minister of Natural Resources until his own death in 1981).

Other appointments went to Oginga Odinga (whom he named Vice-President for a while until he fell out of favour), Tom Mboya (Minister for Home Affairs), Achieng Oneko, Njoroge Mungai (Foreign Affairs), Charles Njonjo (Attorney-General), James Gichuru (Minister of Defence) and many others who had been there for him during his times of trials and tribulations.

As for the rest of the Koinange family, many were appointed to civil service positions as Provincial Commissioners, District Commissioners, and heads of institutions of higher learning, while others were awarded company chairmanships, directorships and ambassadorships.

Over three and a half decades after his death, the Koinange family is today a shadow of what it once was. Many of the chief's children (second generation) became entangled in vicious and sometimes brutal and ugly legal fights over who would inherit the family land. For a while this became front-page news, leading many to quip that the old Koinange was probably turning in his grave at the way his name was being splashed across national headlines. It is ironic that the same land the chief fought so hard to keep from the colonialists was being fought over by his children.

In the end, only history can judge what people such as Koinange-wa-Mbiyu stood for and accomplished. As with most things in life, there are various schools of thought on how he should be judged. Some are of the notion that Koinange was a captive of the colonial situation, not its master. To others, he was a portrait of 'the contradictions of collaboration'; but the majority will agree that he was first and foremost, *Kikuyu Karinga*, pure and independent Kikuyu, who tried more than anyone else to obtain the return of lands lost to white settlement while attempting to remedy the injustices and inequalities that the colonial system imposed on his people. As Fenner Brockway summed it up:

'He loved people of all races, longed for their co-operation, and had a spiritual beauty which lifted him above all but a few. His body at least lies under a tree on the farm he loved.'[7]

Marshall Clough in his book, *Fighting Both Sides*, aptly describes the impact left by this diminutive man who walked tall among his peers:

'Koinange is remembered with deep affection throughout Kiambu and beyond for his hospitality, honesty, and advocacy of his people's cause. The opinion of a fellow chief – "You cannot find anyone better than Koinange" – is echoed by many others. Liked by his European superiors yet popular with his people; progressive but friendly with traditional Kikuyu; a leader of moderates respected by his militant opponents: Koinange was a remarkable conciliator and reconciler of opposites. But first and foremost, he was a Kikuyu patriot.'[8]

Unlike many who came after him, Koinange thought of others first and foremost, sometimes at the expense of members of his own family, and for that alone the diminutive chief stands tall among giants of the freedom struggle. His place in history is reserved, his name uttered in the same breath as that of freedom heroes such as Kimathi, Kenyatta, Kubai, Odinga, Oneko, Ngala, Muthoni, Mwariama and the many other martyrs who make us proud to be Kenyans, proud to be from this land not only referred to as the cradle of mankind, but also the cradle of the independent struggle for *Uhuru*.

ENDNOTES

Chapter 1

1. Marshall S. Clough, *Fighting Both Sides* (page 3). University of Colorado Press, 1990.
2. Marshall S. Clough, *Fighting Both Sides* (page 5).
3. Jomo Kenyatta, *My People of Gikuyu* (page 3). First published by United Society for Christian Literature, Lutterworth Press, 1942 and later by Oxford University Press, 1966.
4. Jomo Kenyatta, *Facing Mount Kenya* (page 6). Vintage Books, 1965.
5. Richard Cox, *Kenyatta's Country*. Hutchinson and Co Ltd, 1965.
6. Jomo Kenyatta, *My People of Gikuyu* (page 4). First published by United Society for Christian Literature, Lutterworth Press, 1942 and later by Oxford University Press, 1966.

Chapter 2

1. Joyce Kagendo Koinange (Koinange's third wife) in an interview, December, 1993.
2. Marshall S. Clough, *Koinange-wa-Mbiyu: Mediator and Patriot* in *Biographical Essays on Imperialism and Collaboration in Colonial Kenya*, ed B. E. Kipkofir, Nairobi: Kenya Literature Bureau, 1980 (page 73).
3. Joyce Kagendo Koinange (Koinange's third wife) interview, December, 1993.
4. Ibid.
5. Ralph Bunche Jr. 1938 diaries located in the University of California, Los Angeles archives (page 17).

6. Ibid. (page 19).
7. Ibid. (page 23).
8. Ralph Bunche Jr. recorded testimony on cine camera at Githiga village, Kiambu, 1938.

Chapter 3

1. Ralph Bunche Jr.1938 diaries located in the University of California, Los Angeles archives, (page 23).
2. Joyce Kagendo Koinange (Koinange's third wife) in an interview, December, 1993.

Chapter 4

1. Charles Millar, *The Lunatic Express*. Macmillan, 1971
2. Jeremy Murray-Brown, *Kenyatta* (page 24). Dutton, 1973.
3. Ralph Bunche Jr. 1938 diaries located in the University of California, Los Angeles archives (page 25).
4. Jeremy Murray-Brown, *Kenyatta* (page 32). Dutton.1973.
5. Ralph Bunche Jr. 1938 diaries located in the University of California, Los Angeles archives (page 41).
6. Ibid. (page 43).
7. Marshall S. Clough, *Koinange-wa-Mbiyu: Mediator & Patriot*. Biographical essay.
8. Ibid.
9. Ralph Bunche Jr. 1938 diaries located in the University of California, Los Angeles archives (page 27).
10. Joyce Kagendo Koinange (Koinange's third wife) in an interview, 1993.
11. Ralph Bunche Jr. 1938 diaries located in the University of California, Los Angeles archives (page 33).
12. L. S. B. Leakey, *The Southern Kikuyu before 1903*. Vol 1. London. Academic Press, 1977 (page 57).
13. Fenner Brockway, *African Journeys* (page 17). Victor Gollancz, London.1955.
14. Kenya National Archives. District Commissioner's notes (page 13), 1925.
15. Ralph Bunche Jr. 1938 diaries located in the University of California, Los Angeles archives (page 27).

Chapter 5

1. Carl Rosberg & John Nottingham, *The Myth of Mau Mau* (page 142). Frederick A. Praeger Publishers, New York and Pall Mall Press, London, 1966.
2. Harry Thuku with assistance from Kenneth King (page 40), Oxford University Press.
3. Marshall S. Clough, *Fighting Two Sides* (page 89) University of Colorado Press, 1990.
4. Marshall S. Clough, *Fighting Two Sides* (page 67). University of Colorado Press, 1990.
5. Marshall S. Clough, *Fighting Two Sides* (page 73). University of Colorado Press, 1990.
6. Ibid. (page 87).
7. Carl Rosberg & John Nottingham, *The Myth of Mau Mau* (page 242). Frederick A. Praeger Publishers, New York and Pall Mall Press, London, 1966.
8. Jeremy Murray-Brown, *Kenyatta* (page 201).
9. Ibid. (page 210).
10. Ibid. (page 212).
11. Ibid. (page 223).

Chapter 6

1. Jeremy Murray-Brown, *Kenyatta* (page 165). Dutton, 1973.
2. Marshall S. Clough, *Fighting Two Sides* (page 85) University of Colorado Press, 1990.
3. Ibid.
4. Harry Thuku with assistance from Kenneth King (page 45). Oxford University Press, 1970.
5. Editorial from Newspaper, *Muiguithania*, 1929. No. 12 (May 1929). KIA DC/MKs/10B 13/1.
6. Harry Thuku with assistance from Kenneth King. Oxford University Press, 1970.
7. Marshall S. Clough, *Koinange-wa-Mbiyu: Mediator and Patriot*, an essay (page 155), 1982.
8. Ralph Bunche Jr. 1938 diaries located in the University of California, Los Angeles archives (page 33).
9. *New York Times*, newspaper headline dated 29 April 1931. (obtained from the university of California, Los Angeles Archives).
10. Jeremy Murray-Brown, *Kenyatta* (page 237).

11. Fenner Brockway, *African Journeys* (page 128). Victor Gollancz, London, 1955.
12. H. E. Lambert. *The Chief's Character Book*. KBU/11/1.
13. Ralph Bunche Jr. 1938 diaries located in the University of California, Los Angeles archives (page 72).
14. Marshall S. Clough, *Fighting Two Sides* (page 159).
15. Ralph Bunche Jr. 1938 diaries located in the University of California, Los Angeles archives (page 19).

Chapter 7

1. Ralph Bunche Jr. 1938 diaries located in the University of California, Los Angeles archives (page 31).
2. Hampton Institute Guidance Counsellor Report, 1927.
3. Hampton Institute Guidance Counsellor Report. 1927.
4. Hampton Institute Senior Yearbook. Class of 1931.
5. Lettter written by Yale President, Charles T. Ioram to Hampton Institute President, Arthur Howe in 1936.
6. Brian Urquhart, *Ralph Bunche Jr – An American Life* (page 19). WW Norton & Co. New York, 1993.
7. Ralph Bunche Jr. 1938 diaries located in the University of California, Los Angeles archives (page 64).
8. Ibid (page 37).
9. Ibid (page 49).
10. Brian Urquhart, *Ralph Bunche Jr – An American Life* (page 117).
11. Ambu Patel, *Struggle for Release Jomo and His Colleagues* (page 16). New Kenya Publishers, Nairobi, 1960.
12. Jeremy Murray-Brown, *Kenyatta* (page 262).
13. Ambu Patel, *Struggle for Release Jomo and His Colleagues* (page 26). New Kenya Publishers, Nairobi, 1960.
14. Jeremy Murray-Brown, *Kenyatta* (page 239).
15. Ambu Patel, *Struggle for Release Jomo and His Colleagues* (page 22). New Kenya Publishers, Nairobi, 1960.
16. Jeremy Murray-Brown, *Kenyatta* (page 249).
17. Carl Rosberg & John Nottingham, *The Myth of Mau Mau* (page 235).
18. Kenya National Archives, District Commissioner, 1925.
19. Marshall S. Clough, *Koinange: Mediator & Patriot*.

Chapter 8

1. Ambu Patel, *Struggle for Release Jomo and His Colleagues* (page 25). New Kenya Publishers, Nairobi, 1961.
2. Jeremy Murray-Brown, *Kenyatta* (page 222).
3. Peter Mbiyu Koinange, *The People of Kenya Speak for Themselves* (page 43).
4. Karari Njama & Donald Barnett, *Mau Mau From Within* (page 69). Monthly review Press, 1970.
5. Robert B. Edgerton, *Mau Mau – An African Crucible* (page 217).
6. Ibid. (page 229).

Chapter 9

1. Carl Rosberg & John Nottingham. *The Myth of Mau Mau* (page 237).
2. Robert B. Edgerton, *Mau Mau- An African Crucible* (page 177).
3. Jeremy Murray-Brown, *Kenyatta* (page 192).
4. Ibid. (page 199).
5. Carl Rosberg & John Nottingham. *The Myth of Mau Mau* (page 232).
6. Robert B. Edgerton, *Mau Mau- An African Crucible* (page 187).
7. Carl Rosberg & John Nottingham. *The Myth of Mau Mau* (page 254).
8. Ibid. (page 272).
9. Ibid. (page 273).
10. Kenya National Archives. District Commissioner, 1952.
11. Robert B. Edgerton, *Mau Mau- An African Crucible* (page 253).

Chapter 10

1. Pauline Njogu (wife of John Westley Mbiyu) testimony, December, 1993.
2. Kenya National Archives, KNA/DC/53/1/3.
3. Robert B. Edgerton, *Mau Mau- An African Crucible* (page 87).
4. Fenner Brockway, *Outside The Right* (page 109). George Allen & Unwin Ltd, 1959.
5. Margaret Wangui Koinange testimony, May, 1997.
6. Fenner Brockway, *Outside The Right* (page 67). George Allen & Unwin Ltd, 1959.
7. H. E. Lambert, *The Chief's Character Book*. KBU/63/2/1.
8. Ibid.

Chapter 11
1. Ambu Patel, *Struggle for Release Jomo and His Colleagues* (page 11). New Kenya Publishers, Nairobi, 1960.
2. Pauline Njogu testimony, December, 1993.
3. Ibid.
4. Joseph Karuga Koinange interview, August, 1998.
5. *East African Standard* excerpt, 31 July 1960.
6. Arthur Koinange interview, December, 1993.
7. Fenner Brockway, *Outside The Right* (page 103).
8. Marshall S. Clough, *Fighting Two Sides* (page 96).

BIBLIOGRAPHY

Books

Barnett, Donald L., & Karari Njama, *Mau Mau from Within*. New York: Monthly Review Press, 1966:
Brockway, Fenner, *Outside The Right*. George Allen & Unwin Ltd, London, 1970.
Brockway, Fenner, *African Journeys*. London Gollancz, 1955.
Clough, Marshall. S., *Fighting Two Sides*. University Press of Colorado, 1990.
Cox, Richard, *Kenyatta's Country*. Hutchinson & Co. London, 1965.
Edgerton, Robert. B., *Mau Mau – An African Crucible*. The Free Press, New York & Collier Macmillan, London, 1989.
Furedi, Frank, *The Mau Mau War in Perspective*. Heinemann, Kenya Ltd, 1990.
Kenyatta. Mzee Jomo, *My People of Kikuyu*. Oxford University Press.
Koinange, Peter Mbiyu, *The People of Kenya Speak for Themselves*. Detroit Press, 1950.
Leakey, L. S. B., *The Southern Kikuyu Before 1903. Vol 1*. London Academic Press, 1977.
Murray-Brown, Jeremy, *Kenyatta*. E. P. Dutton & Co. Inc., New York, 1973.
Patel, Ambu. H., *Struggle for Release Jomo & His Colleagues*. New Kenya Publishers, 1960.
Rosberg, Carl & Nottingham, John, *The Myth of Mau Mau*. Frederick A. Praeger Publishers, New York & Pall Mall Press, London, 1966.
Stoneham, C. T., *Mau Mau*. London Museum Press, 1953.
Thuku, Harry with assistance from Kenneth King. *An Autobiography*. Oxford University Press, Nairobi, Kenya, 1970.

Newspapers

Muigwithania, May 1929.
Sunday Worker, January 1930.
New York Times, April 1931.
East African Standard, July 1960.

GLOSSARY

Andu A Ndemwa Ithatu: People of the three letters.

Arume: The men of the tribe.

Athamaki: Prominent individuals in pre-colonial times, outstanding in warfare, in council, or in judgment.

Atumia: The women of the tribe

Baraza: A gathering of people, usually in an open place.

Boma: Homestead.

Dawa: medicine, or concoction of sorts.

Gichukia: popular dance done by circumcised boys.

Githaka: (Kikuyu) A plot of land usually intended for cultivation.

Githono: Hut built specially for the initiates being circumcised.

Gwithamba: to bathe oneself or immerse in water.

Hukoro: Traditional Gikuyu sacrifice usually performed to ward-off evil spirits.

Irio: Traditional Gikuyu food usually consists of maize, green beans, potatoes and spinach or other green leaves all mashed together.

Irua: The actual circumcision act.

Ithaka: basic term for land belonging to someone.

Ithako: play fighting usually performed by boys.

Jamhuri: Literally means republic (Jamhuri-ya-Kenya – Republic of Kenya).

Johi: traditonal beer.

Kahiu-ga-Kuruithia: The knife used in a circumcision ceremony.

Karing'a: Pure or true; the term used by those who refused to abandon such things as female circumcision.

Kavirondo: Another name for the Luo tribe, situated mostly around Lake Victoria.

Kiama: The traditional council of elders, or the Kikuyu court during the colonial period.

Kienjeku: Koinange-wa-Mbiyu's circumcision year or age-group.

Kipande: The dreaded ID book or registration system that all Africans had to carry around showing who, what and where they were from.

Kirigo: name given to girls who were never circumcised.

Kugandia: To make numb by using a local anesthetic.

Kunanga: The Kikuyu verb meaning to break or to solve (as in disputes). Legend has it this is where the name Koinange originated.

Madaraka: Internal or self-government.

Mahoroga: leaves of the banana plant.

Mahoroha: leaves of a sweet-smelling plant.

Mararia: leaves of a creeper.

Mbari: A Kikuyu lineage.

Mnyapara: Title used for a Headman during the colonial period.

Muchagachugu: special root tuber.

Mugikuyu (pl Agikuyu): People of the Gikuyu or Kikuyu tribe.

Mugumo: Fig Tree, considered a Gikuyu blessing.

Muigwithania: Name of Newspaper which Kenyatta wrote his many articles. Literally means Reconciler or one who brings together.

Mukuyu: type of fig tree.

Muma: Oath-taking.

Mundumugo: Gikuyu traditional witch doctor or medicine man.

Muruithia-wa-Ihii: Man who performs circumcision on boys.

Mutorireo: whistle-blowing as practices by herd boys.

Mwene Nyaga: The traditional God of the Gikuyu people who according to folk lore, lives somewhere on Mount Kenya.

Ndirii: dances between boys and girls.

Ngocho: popular dance done by uncircumcised boys.

Njunge: Age-group or riika older than that of Kienjeku (Koinange-wa-Mbiyu's).

Riika: An individual's circumcision year or age-group.

Ruiga: Bride price or lobola.

Rwenji: razor

Shamba: (Kiswahili) A plot of land.

Thenge: Billy goat.

Uchoro: Gikuyu gruel or porridge.

Ugimbi: Grain from which a traditional Gikuyu gruel is made.

Uhuru: Freedom or independence.

14 DEC 2000
B7
F1 5/05